GERMANY

GERMANY

Baden-Württemberg
Bavaria
Berlin
Brandenburg
Bremen

Hamburg
Hesse
Lower Saxony
Mecklenburg-Lower Pomerania
North Rhine-Westphalia
Rhineland-Palatinate

Saarland
Saxony
Saxony-Anhalt
Schleswig-Holstein
Thuringia

Text:
Rudolf Walter Leonhardt

Photographs:
Josef H. Neumann

BUCHER

Concept: Axel Schenck
Translation: John Ormrod
Editor: Barbara Hopkinson
Graphic Design: Ludwig Kaiser
Production editor: Angelika Kerscher

© 1991 by Verlag C. J. Bucher GmbH,
Munich and Berlin
All rights reserved
Reproduction of photographs by
Heidelberger Klischee, Heidelberg.
Printed by Passavia, Passau.
Bound by Conzella, Munich.
ISBN 3 7658 0691 9

Contents

- 6   Richard von Weizsäcker:
Thoughts on the Identity of the Germans
- 9   Rudolf Walter Leonhardt:
Germany in Search of Itself

Illustrations:
- 12   Chapter 1: The Far North
- 24   Chapter 2: The German Coastline
- 40   Chapter 3: The Baltic Coast from Wismar to Usedom
- 52   Chapter 4: In the Plain
- 64   Chapter 5: The Lakelands of Mecklenburg
- 76   Chapter 6: Berlin, Brandenburg and the Spree Forest
- 92   Chapter 7: The Hercynian Mountains
- 108   Chapter 8: The Ruhr District and the Münsterland
- 120   Chapter 9: Saxony
- 132   Chapter 10: Thuringia, Dresden and the River Elbe
- 145   From the Baltic to Bavaria, from Cologne to Dresden. Literary Accounts of the German Regions
- 148   Germany in Old Photographs, 1850-1920
Chapter 11: From Bremen to Stralsund
- 168   Germany in Old Photographs, 1850-1930
Chapter 12: From Berlin to Chemnitz
- 188   Chapter 13: Festivities
- 204   Germany in Old Photographs, 1850-1920
Chapter 14: From Cologne to Munich
- 224   Chapter 15: Up the Rhine
- 236   Chapter 16: On the Moselle and Main
- 248   Chapter 17: Franconia
- 260   Chapter 18: Towns and Castles in Baden, Württemberg and the Palatinate
- 276   Chapter 19: In Upper and Lower Bavaria

Appendix:
- 295   Map
- 296   Index
- 299   List of Sources and Illustrations

Richard von Weizsäcker
Thoughts on the Identity of the Germans

Nations which are uncertain of their relationship to the past often find it difficult to cope with the present: their identity becomes problematical.

Culture has played a leading role in constituting the Germans' sense of identity. It was through the medium of culture that a German national awareness first emerged in the eighteenth century, not as a political movement, but as a striving for intellectual and cultural autonomy, for independence from France. This is exemplified in Lessing's proposals for a national theatre and Herder's idea of a national culture.

The great achievements of German classical philosophy and literature, of Kant and Goethe, found worldwide recognition. They gave the Germans a sense of belonging to a common culture, one which was respected by other nations. Being German was something to be proud of. However, for us Germans, the relationship between politics and culture has often been a highly problematical issue. As early as 1794, Schiller wrote:

"Germany? But where does it lie?

I know not where to find the land. Where the world of books begins, that of politics ends."

The poet Hölderlin called the Germans "poor in deed and rich in ideas".

Ideas are not tied to a specific place and time: they are free to wander back and forth at will, but action is rooted in the here and now. Nietzsche said: "The Germans have a past and a distant future, but no present." Thomas Mann spoke of German spirituality, of the "musicality of the soul", as the most attractive feature of the national character. But he also pointed to the German propensity for mysticism, the enemy of clarity, and criticized the apolitical nature of the German mind.

These are subjective opinions. I do not cite them in order to prove the existence of some "typically" German set of characteristics. The point I wish to make concerning culture is this: whenever we Germans have taken culture seriously and have sought to follow our own cultural path, we have not only been accepted by others, but we have also acted in our own best interests. This still holds good today.

The emphasis on culture does not imply a rejection of the age of technology: still less does it entail the adoption of an apolitical attitude. Culture is a way of life. Hence culture is also politics. Culture, seen as a way of life, is perhaps the most authentic form of politics. Culture reinforces our sense of selfhood, especially where divisions between political and social systems impose a strain on our identity.

Let us return to the political history of Germany. At the time of the Napoleonic Wars, the emergent national awareness of the Germans became the driving force of a movement for political liberation. The search for a national identity was no longer confined to Lessing's national theatre: it also took on a political dimension. Following the defeat of the democratic movement which established the first all-German parliament at the Paulskirche in 1848, and the war of 1866 which drove Austria out of the German League, Bismarck founded the Second Empire in 1871. He envisioned a Germany which would form a bridge and act as a mediator between east and west.

Meanwhile, however, the nationalism of the European peoples had taken on a dangerous slant. One nation looked down on another, glorifying its own image and deprecating that of its neighbours. Overblown national pride intensified the lust for power. Industrialization proceeded apace, and the era of colonialism began.

After Bismarck's resignation, the dam burst, and Germany lost all sense of moderation. As a latecomer to nationalism, the country went full-steam ahead in a dangerous effort to catch up on its rivals. By launching an attack on the rest of the world, Germany inadvertently united its neighbours into an overwhelmingly powerful grand coalition. At the end of the First World War, Germany was defeated and additionally humiliated by the terms of the Treaty of Versailles.

In the years which followed, responsible people in France and Germany endeavoured to secure peace, but they were unable to prevail over the forces of nationalism, which remained unbowed. Germany saw the re-emergence of an extreme form of nationalism which fed on social unrest and economic hardship.

Hitler elevated the German nation to the status of a supreme value. He told his countrymen that as members of the Teutonic race, they had a God-given right to rule the world. The consequence was violence and world war. In the countries occupied by the German armies, Jews and others were rounded up and murdered. The Holocaust took its terrible course. Everywhere, including Germany itself, there was genocide, extermination and unparalleled hatred, death and immeasurable suffering. Germany was destroyed and conquered, occupied and partitioned. In the aftermath of all this, what does the word "German" mean?

Germany had plumbed the depths of violence and guilt. Our energies had been exhausted by the effort of the terrible war. We had been liberated from the iniquitous regime of National Socialism. But for many of us, the suffering was not yet over. There followed the expulsion by force of innocent people from the regions which had been their home for centuries.

In those days, it was difficult to be a German. The Germans were in fundamental dissent with themselves. How could things have been otherwise, after all that had happened, after all the lost illusions, the injustice, the dishonesty, the careless way in which we had wrapped ourself in ignorance and disregarded the dictates of our conscience?

But the history of Germany did not come to an end in 1945. For nearly four decades, a liberal democracy has existed on German soil. This too is part of our history: a part which is good. Today, when people in other countries speak of the Germans, they also think of freedom, social justice and democracy.

Our democracy has its faults like any other. Some critics trace these faults back to typically German characteristics. But such arguments do not lead very far. Our particular set of experiences and memories is not only a burden: it also yields helpful insights which may protect us from further mistakes. We have a more extensive experience than almost any other people of dictatorship, war and injustice.

This is a particularly difficult chapter in our history, in a heritage which has both its lighter and its darker sides. But the better we understand it and preserve its memory, unambiguously accepting responsibility for its consequences, the less our identity will be threatened by crises arising from the past. By coming to terms with the past, we enhance our self-understanding and help our neighbours to understand us as well.

Many people say: "All this eternal harping on the past – it has nothing to do with us and we don't want to be bothered with it." But I believe that the reverse is true. The past only becomes a burden when we turn our heads and look away. By openly confronting it, we lighten the burden and make it easier for ourselves to cope with the tasks of the present. (*Speech delivered on 8 June 1985 at the 21st Convention of the German Protestant Church in Düsseldorf*)

For as long as I can remember, I have never experienced a moment such as this, when the whole world shared in the joy which we felt on being reunited. In my lifetime, the interest of other countries in Germany has often been accompanied by very different feelings. We would still do well not to lose sight of the yardstick by which our neighbours judge us.

But the scenes we have witnessed recently at the Brandenburg Gate in Berlin, and all over Germany, have united the hearts of the whole world. Journalists from the Soviet Union, the Mayor of Jerusalem, western heads of state and many other people have written to me or telephoned to express the joy which they also feel. People have been brought closer together by a common surge of emotion.

How did these events come about? For the first time in European history we have seen a revolution which is a pure expression of popular will, a truly democratic revolution.

In the GDR the longing for freedom has triumphed without violence. It became an irresistible force. People were no longer afraid. Their faith in peace was renewed, and the rule of law was seen as the best form of state security; thus there were lighted candles in front of the Stasi buildings and flowers for the police.

The movement began in the churches, the only public places which were free of state interference. For several years, people had been assembling regularly to pray for peace, to keep alive the flame of hope and vigilance.

We do not believe in the doctrine of Germany as a country with a special destiny, leading us down the path of isolation. Naturally, the ties between the East and West Germans are closer than those which link us with other Europeans. We Germans are one people. But at the same time we are all preparing for the great step forward into a united Europe whose member countries will help one another to develop and progress. (*Christmas radio and television address on 24 and 25 December 1989*)

European unity does not mean unity under a single state or a uniform social system: it means pursuing a common path of humanity and historical progress. In this sense, the German question is a task which concerns Europe as a whole...

Shortly after the end of the Second World War, the French poet Paul Claudel wrote the following words concerning the Germans:

"The role of Germany is not to divide peoples but to bring them together, to create agreement and make all the surrounding nations realize that they cannot exist without each other."

This idea that the peoples of Europe depend on one another constitutes a grand challenge which we can face with confidence. In doing so, we may benefit precisely from our troubled history and the division of our country.

The way forward into the future is uncertain. It is at once dark and open. It is up to us to determine its direction. We are all free men and women. It is our task to give the word "German" a meaning with which we ourselves and the rest of the world can live happily and in peace. (*Speech delivered on 8 June 1985 at the 21st Convention of the German Protestant Church in Düsseldorf*)

Rudolf Walter Leonhardt
Germany in Search of Itself

Is it permissible to focus on the attractive features of a country about which one could say so many uncomplimentary things? Isn't this a misrepresentation, a false colouring of the truth? The photographs in this book do not gloss over reality: they merely leave out certain things which we considered uninteresting as subjects for the camera, such as the opencast lignite mines around Böhlen and the bleak, barrack-like housing estates of Bremen. In fact, barracks and other things of a military nature do not feature here at all.

We don't share the view of the German Idealist thinkers that only the beautiful is true. But we are even less inclined to accept the converse opinion that beauty is inevitably false. Where more sombre tones are called for, we think that they should appear in the text, not in the pictures. The main purpose of the photographs in this book is to point out the beauties of nature and culture with which Germany is so richly endowed and which are so quintessentially "German".

There is a strange discrepancy between the natural beauty of Germany and the country's history and supposed national character. Over the centuries, many things have been said about the Germans, but they have rarely been called "charming", "graceful", "restrained" or "harmonious". Yet these are precisely the typical attributes of the German landscape. Germany has no breathtaking Grand Canyons or majestic Mount Everests; its coastline is unspectacular and its climate temperate: the storms are not wild, the summers are not scorching, and the winters are seldom severe. The characteristic charm and harmonious beauty of the German landscape is to be found in the gentle wooded slopes of the Harz mountains and the Black Forest, in the pleasant valleys of the Moselle and the Havel, in the sleepy lakelands of southern Bavaria and Mecklenburg.

In the realm of culture, beauty is invariably equated with age. There are good reasons for this, but the consequences are somewhat peculiar. People who are unsure of their own style tend, quite rightly, to prize things which have been hallowed by past generations, often ascribing to them a merit which they do not really have. (This, in turn, opens up possibilities for the professional iconoclasts.) One wonders if there has ever been a time which was less confident than our own of its cultural style.

It would seem, too, that people experience a thrill of reverence when they see something old and imagine: this house or this gate was already standing before I was even thought of, and it will still be there long after I have been forgotten. In old buildings, the striving for continuity, beyond the life-span of the individual, takes on concrete form, and this is the reason why we prize them so highly.

The buildings which we today regard as beautiful were created by our forebears – at any rate, by those of them who held the reins of power – as a manifestation of their own identity, as a token of resistance, or in order to gain prestige and improve their social standing by creating and collecting art. These were the purposes which inspired the building of houses and castles, fortresses and city walls, churches and cathedrals, theatres and museums. Standing in this cultural landscape, we feel strangely lost. These remnants of the past appear to have little real connection with our own lives: we see them as tourist attractions, mere illusions for leisure consumption only. But the appearance is deceptive. In our collective subconscious, this cultural heritage, together with the beauties of nature, constitutes what we really mean when we think of "Germany".

Far more controversy surrounds the elements which the twentieth century has added, in the literal, visual sense, to this image of Germany: motorway junctions and airports, shipyards and factories. Are these things beautiful? In some cases we can say "yes", because we accept functional beauty as a harmonious reconciliation of ends with means. But regardless of whether it is beautiful or ugly, useful or objectionable, there is something about this modern industrial landscape which discourages us from paying it excessive homage. Even if one's aim is to show the modern face of Germany, one is well-advised to use pictures of industry sparingly, since there is little visible difference between an airport in Frankfurt and an airport in San Francisco, and only experts can distinguish a car factory in Stuttgart from its counterpart in Turin or Detroit. Like luxury hotels, industrial landscapes are the same the world over: they all fulfil much the same functions. Political ideologies, social conflicts and national events of immediate topical interest are also difficult to incorporate in a picture which would have any permanence: within a year it would be outdated and in need of correction.

Whatever "Germany" may mean to me or any other German, or to a foreigner, the things which we find attractive about it do not change all that quickly.

Instead, our Germany comprises a somewhat shadowy history of the German mind, which cannot be represented in visual terms, and a set of sensory perceptions which broadly correspond to those which are reproduced here, enabling the reader to recreate them in his own imagination.

A Beautiful Fiction

Germany is a beautiful fiction. But whenever the Germans began to take this fiction seriously, in terms of *Realpolitik*, it promptly ceased to be beautiful. Since the breakup of the Holy Roman Empire, the longest period for which "Germany" existed as a nation-state whose actual territorial boundaries justified its name, was forty-seven years, from 1871 to 1918. It is impossible to identify "Germany" on the political map in the way that one can point out France or Great Britain. When speaking of Germany in a political context, we have accustomed ourselves, for good reasons, to appending the rider "in the borders of" 1871, 1918, 1937, 1949 or 1990. But "Germany" apparently exists, as a concept to which fewer prejudices are attached the more firmly one refrains from defining it. The vaguer the definition, the clearer the contours of the country paradoxically become; contours, however, which are more distinctly visible to someone living in Tokyo or Boston than to a citizen of Leipzig or Hamburg.

My own children, who grew up in Hamburg, know literally nothing about Leipzig. My relatives in Leipzig are somewhat older, but they too know very little about Hamburg. And this state of affairs, which has persisted for forty years, is not going to change overnight. But for my French and English cousins, Leipzig and Hamburg have always been cities belonging to more or less the same country, which they call "Allemagne" or "Germany", occasionally tacking on an "East" or "West" when they are trying to be particularly accurate.

The country which we may and shall call "Germany" is the product of 2,000 years of history. All stories have to begin somewhere: the history of Germany begins with the Teutonic tribes which subdued the Roman armies in the first centuries A.D. and were themselves subdued by Roman civilization. The first German "monuments", the stone circles in Teutoburg Forest and the Porta Nigra in Trier, date

Off to the seaside – or at least to the photographer's studio, where this turn-of-the-century German family is seen posing with one of the recently-invented wicker beach chairs, a painted backdrop showing the North Sea, and a real bucket and spade.

The Far North

Near Norddorf on the island of Amrum
A striking composition of sea, sand, water and a boundless horizon.

Helgoland
The island of red cliffs in the German Bay lies outside German Customs jurisdiction and has a long and still lively tradition as a destination for day-trippers and holiday-makers.

Greetsiel in East Friesland
This harbour town on the Leybucht preserved the typical charm of an old Frisian fishing village thanks to tradition-conscious local inhabitants who devote considerable effort to restoration.

Near Worpswede
Forest house near Worpswede, formerly home to a colony of artists, among them the painters Becker-Modersohn, Mackensen, Modersohn, Ende, Overbeck and Vogeler.

The Roland in Bremen
Roland, a legendary figure closely linked with Charlemagne, is the emblem of the Hanseatic town of Bremen. Here, and in many other towns of Northern and Central Germany, the marketplaces are adorned with wooden or stone statues of Roland.

back to this period: they still stand today.

Ever since then, confusion has been the inevitable outcome of all attempts at establishing a nation-state between a relatively stable western border, lying somewhere between Verdun and Trier, which has fluctuated very little over the years, and an extremely weak eastern border which has never been more than a provisional dividing line between the German and the Slav empires. In this context, the border of the GDR, protected by barbed wire and minefields, could be seen as a desperate attempt to guarantee stability in the East on a long-term basis.

These days determining the northern and southern borders of "Germany" appears to be relatively easy. The difficulties only begin when one takes a closer look at the history of the northernmost and southernmost German regions: Schleswig-Holstein and South Tyrol. Since our Scandinavian neighbours are peace-loving people, we have forgotten the explosiveness of the "Schleswig-Holstein Question": it is remembered only by historians. And the "problem" of Tyrol, insofar as it still persists, is no longer a German but an Austrian problem. The political solution adopted for Tyrol became a model for other countries: a partition was established between the north and south, as later happened in Korea, Yemen and Vietnam.

"From the Maas to the Memel, from the Adige to the Belt": these were the borders of Germany as seen by the poet Hoffmann von Fallersleben, who in 1841 composed a German national anthem which, much to his chagrin, no one wanted to sing. He gave it the ambitious title "Song of the Germans", but the Germans preferred other songs by the same author: harmless ditties about birds and forests. In 1871, Hoffmann dejectedly complained that his work had been ignored and deemed rubbish.

However, the old gentleman obviously had few dealings with young people, with students and members of the politicized gymnastics clubs known as *Turnvereine*, who were celebrating the reunification of Germany under the leadership of Bismarck by singing Hoffmann's song. The "Song of the Germans" had originally been written in protest against the political fragmentation of Germany into a multitude of small states, not as a hymn to German expansionism. But these young people harnessed it to a new political purpose. It was their sons who are said to have marched into battle in the First World War with the "Song of the Germans" on their lips. On 11 August 1922, Friedrich Ebert, the Social Democratic *Reichspräsident*, officially decreed that Hoffmann's song, set to Haydn's music, would be the anthem of the new Weimar Republic.

Thirty years later, Theodor Heuss, the first President of the Federal Republic of Germany, found it much more difficult to decide on the issue of the national anthem. Some form of anthem was obviously necessary for ceremonies and state receptions. After an exchange of correspondence with Chancellor Adenauer, still a subject of controversy, Heuss finally accepted the Federal government's proposal to reinstate Hoffmann's song as the national anthem. The third verse only was to be sung on state occasions.

Ever since Heuss's decision, academics have argued about the "Song of the Germans", debating whether the first two verses should still be considered as part of the anthem or not. There can be few objections to the second verse, which praises "German women and German loyalty, German wine and German song". But the first verse was and remains unacceptable on three grounds. Firstly it was used in Hitler's Germany as a kind of prelude to the Nazi anthem, the Horst Wessel Song. Secondly it contains the seemingly chauvinist words "Deutschland, Deutschland über alles". And thirdly it took the fiction of "Germany" seriously and attempted to give it a specific political shape.

The Germans' search for a national identity has always been problematic. The Third Reich and its consequences made it impossible for the two ge-

The seaside holiday is a long-established tradition, as is the building of sandcastles such as the one in this photograph from the island of Sylt (ca 1905) which has the added advantage of offering protection from the wind.

nerations to find an identity. Members of the first had a guilty conscience, from which they endeavoured to distance themselves. Members of the second had to distance themselves from their parents. If this had not been the case, one could take a more relaxed attitude and point out that national anthems invariably contain a hint of chauvinism: the anthems of Britain and France are no exception. It should also be remembered that Hoffmann von Fallersleben, a professor from Brunswick, was a liberal democrat who would have no truck with chauvinism: when he wrote the words "Deutschland über alles", he was thinking of the Grand Duchy of Mecklenburg-Schwerin, the Kingdom of Hanover, the Principality of Schwarzburg-Sondershausen and the Grand Duchy of Baden, not of Poland or France.

Nor did the way in which Hoffmann delineated the borders of Germany imply any kind of plan for world conquest. Admittedly, his definition of Germany was less modest than that of his predecessor Walther von der Vogelweide, the German medieval poet who sang of Germany "from the Elbe to the Rhine and to the land of the Magyars". But this was 600 years before Hoffmann, long before the emergence of Prussia. At the time Hoffmann wrote his song, the town of Limburg on the River Maas had just joined the league of German states known as the Deutscher Bund; the Memel formed the border between East Prussia and Lithuania; South Tyrol, whose principal river is the Adige, belonged to Austria, which was also a member of the Deutscher Bund until 1866; and the River Belt ran along the northern border of the Duchy of Schleswig-Holstein, which at that time was the subject of a territorial dispute.

A trip round the harbour (ca 1920). Excursion boats of this kind are still to be found in Hamburg; the open-mouthed land-lubbers are treated to a humorous commentary by the boatman as he takes them on a tour of the port, from which ships sail all over the world.

What made the "Song of the Germans" objectionable was not so much the way that Hoffmann drew the borders as the fact that he drew them at all: his attempt to do so proved rash and premature. These days, the area which we call "Germany" is far smaller.

A Journey to the Other Part of Germany

The Germans tried to circumvent the problem of national identity by speaking, quite correctly, not of "Germany", but of the FRG and the GDR. But this cautious terminology could not provide a way out of the dilemma. If we cannot identify "Germany", then what do we mean when we speak of "the Germans"? What is the "German" landscape or "German" art?

Is there such a thing as "German" history or the "German language": do they still exist as definite concepts, or have they been reinstated as such by the events of 1990? Weren't the "late capitalist" Federal Republic and the "socialist" GDR antitheses which tore apart the very meaning of everything which we call "German"?

When I, a citizen of the Federal Republic, travelled to the GDR to visit the small town where I went to school forty years ago, I entered another world. I had to apply for a visa, as if I were crossing the Atlantic, and it was not a foregone conclusion that my application would be granted. It was a journey of 400 kilometres, which I would normally make by car. Instead, I bought a plane ticket to Berlin: I was prohibited from using my car to return to the small town to which I owed my so-called classical education.

The German Coastline

Beach near Travemünde
A perfect seaside scene near Travemünde, the world-famous Baltic spa. Since 1913 it has belonged administratively to the Hanseatic town of Lübeck.

On the island of Amrum
With its wicker beach chairs, fine sand and North Sea tides, the North Frisian island of Amrum is an attractive resort for a bathing holiday.

Neustadt in Holstein
Sandwiched between the bay of Lübeck and a salt-water lake, Neustadt was a lively shipping and mercantile centre in the 19th century.

Husum
Theodor Storm's "grey town on the sea" is situated where the areas of "Marsch" and "Geest" meet, and is the cultural and economic hub of North Friesland.

Glücksburg Castle near Flensburg
Erected in 1587 under Duke Johann the Younger, this Renaissance castle with moat is now a museum.

House on the Halligen island of Langeness
Only nine of the "Marsch" islands in the North Frisian mudflats are inhabited today and possess accommodation that can withstand the storm tides.

Flensburg
Impressions of the harbour in Flensburg, which has the largest naval yards on the Flensburger Förde. Today Flensburg is an important industrial centre.

Schleswig
This part of the country town of Schleswig has a surprisingly rural appearance.

Gottorf Castle, Schleswig
Gottorf Castle, seat of the Dukes of Schleswig-Holstein since 1544, possesses a sumptuously decorated chapel and is considered one of the best examples of Renaissance architecture in Northern Germany.

Between Neustadt on the Baltic and Heiligenhafen
Charming river views near Brodau.

In the Holsteinische Schweiz
The morainal landscape between Eutin and Plön with its many woods and lakes is a popular recreational area.

Lübeck
The emblem of Lübeck, the oldest and formerly most powerful Hanseatic town, is the Holstentor. In marzipan this city gate has made its mark all over the world.

Travemünde
View of the harbour at Travemünde, the largest port for passenger traffi in Europe.

Is this now all water under the bridge, a minor error of history, or a major blunder committed by the Soviet Union? I think not. The victors of the Second World War partitioned Germany, but the estrangement between the FRG and the GDR was produced by the Germans themselves. It will take many years to abolish the distinction between the "Wessies" and the "Ossies", the Westerners and the Easterners. Hence I intend to continue my account of my journey from the West to the East. The wall has now come down, but the mental barriers will remain for some time to come.

At Zoo station on the S-Bahn line, I said farewell to the familiar world of the West and boarded one of the trains which were boycotted for years by many West Berliners because they belonged to the GDR. Between Lehrter Bahnhof and Friedrichstrasse stations, one could look through the board fence and catch an occasional glimpse of the world's ugliest and most closely guarded border. Of course there were practical reasons why the border checkpoint for rail passengers was located in the dimly-lit tunnels and subterranean halls underneath Friedrichstrasse station. But these things alone were not responsible for the mood of gloom which invariably overtook me. Altogether, I must have gone through that checkpoint about fifty times, and each time I felt the crossing to be the most depressing thing that could happen to a German in peacetime.

Up to this point, my story corresponds to the textbook notions of people's feelings on entering a different, entirely strange world. I was not exactly frightened, but I had a sense of being continually threatened. On the other side, I boarded the S-Bahn again and travelled to the Ostbahnhof, which used to be called Schlesischer Bahnhof. It becomes difficult to find one's bearings when the names of so many things have been changed. However, there were a few surprising anomalies: the Deutsche Reichsbahn, for example, had retained its old name. In the meantime, the train to Leipzig has become more attractive, with modern double-decker coaches, but it is neither cleaner nor dirtier than before, and certainly no faster.

The sense of strangeness gradually evaporates. Indeed, many things now appear oddly familiar. The train passes through the sandy heathland of the Mark Brandenburg, stopping in Luckenwalde, Jüterbog and the town of Wittenberg, famous for its association with Martin Luther: it stands on the River Elbe, which connects it with Hamburg. The next station is Bitterfeld, an industrial town whose vast state-owned chemical factory has given it the reputation of being the dirtiest place in Europe. It is also notorious for the "Bitterfeld Resolutions" of 1948, abolishing the freely-elected factory councils, and for the "Bitterfelder Weg", a set of guidelines for the emergence of a truly socialist art which were issued in 1959.

At Delitzsch, just past Bitterfeld, one enters the industrial region of northern Saxony. Many of the towns and villages here have Slavonic names, such as Wiederizsch, Kieritzsch, Nitzschka and Groitzsch. Many of them have also vanished; they have been swallowed up by the giant excavators which dig up lignite coal in the open-cast mines. The coal is then hydrogenated at the huge plants in Leuna and Espenhain, where the air is the vilest I have ever breathed.

The main station at Leipzig, in which the city has always taken great pride, is a familiar landmark on my journey into the past. The next train to the small town where I grew up is due to leave in four hours' time. One never had to wait this long in the past, but such delays are part of an international pattern: the service on branch lines is declining as a result of rationalization. And here too, an international trick helps one to get a taxi. In the GDR, taxis were cheap but hard to come by. I used the same ploy which had stood me in good stead in Hamburg, New York and Moscow. I sat down for a short while in the foyer of a hotel which evidently set great store by its inter-

The Town Hall in Greifswald (ca 1910). Originally a Gothic brick building, it was renovated in the style of the late Renaissance following a fire in the eighteenth century.

national reputation, and ordered a drink. After a few minutes I went over to the desk clerk and addressed him in a friendly tone. He was far too polite to ask whether I was actually a guest at the hotel, and within ten minutes I had a taxi. An hour later I was back in the small town where I went to school.

The Saxon electoral princes who founded the school called it just that: a school (*Schule*). When the principality became a kingdom, the school's name remained unchanged. But then, highly-educated and education-hungry classical scholars came along and changed the name from *Schule* to *Gymnasium*. When King Friedrich August abdicated in November 1918, addressing the famous last words to the cheering crowds, "Ihr seid mir scheene Räbubliganer!" ("A fine lot of republicans you are!"), the name *Gymnasium* was retained. Today, however, the school has become a school again, or, to be more precise, a so-called *weiterführende Oberschule* (higher secondary school). Perhaps the name will soon be changed back to *Gymnasium*. The education of the human race is a somewhat erratic process.

In the centre of small towns such as this, there is invariably a market square with a town hall, and the church is close by. To reward thirsty churchgoers there are generally several inns in the vicinity, the largest of which is usually called the *Ratskeller*. In the Protestant north of Germany, it has long been the custom that some men go to the inn rather than to church. When I was a small boy just starting school, the official name of the square was Friedrich-Ebert-Platz. But the townspeople called it the Marktplatz (Market Square). When the Nazis took over the administration of the small town in 1933, the square

Left: The walled town of Stralsund successfully withstood the siege by the Imperial army under the command of Wallenstein in 1628. The Kütertor, built in 1446, is a symbol of the town's determination to resist aggressors (1910/20).

Right: The heart of the old town in Rostock. The Marienkirche is a brick-built Gothic basilica with a nave and two aisles; among the features which testify to its long history are the altars, the font and the Baroque organ.

was renamed Adolf-Hitler-Platz. The people continued to call it Marktplatz. In 1945 the town was occupied by Soviet troops, and the square was rechristened Stalin-Platz on the orders of the military government. But the people kept on referring to it as Marktplatz, and this is the name they still use. Reflecting political events on the world stage, the name Stalin was later replaced by Karl Marx, but his popularity has also declined: people have stopped naming streets after him.

Entering one of these inns on any day of the week, regardless of whether one has been to church, a warm welcome is found. The people are friendly; looking at them, they could be the same people as those whom I used to see when I was young. Their clothes tell you whether it is a weekday or a Sunday. There has always been the occasional uniform in evidence, but uniforms have never been predominant: they are less than popular in the places where people drink, and conversations tend to become hushed in their presence, apart from disdainful comments such as "He's only a soldier", a remark which I heard again only recently, echoing the very words that people used in the distant past.

In days gone by, the drinkers would doubtless have included one or two convinced Nazis, and later there would have been a handful of fanatical Communists. But these people – the petits gens in their small inns in the small town – are pleasant and friendly. Of course, they are never satisfied with their lot. They never have been. And they are always a little bit afraid: of their wives, their bosses, or the Party. But they are never really frightened, since they don't have all that much to lose. And everyone knows everyone

The Baltic Coast from Wismar to Usedom

Ahlbeck on Usedom
The gleaming white sandy beach, bordered by woods, extends as far as the eye can see. The villages of Heringsdorf, Bansin and Ahlbeck are connected by a promenade and form the tourist centre of Usedom.

Rostock
View of the brick-built churches of St. Peter (centre) and St. Nicholas (right). On the left one sees the River Warnow, with some of the old warehouses, also built in brick.

Rostock, formerly one of the most powerful towns in the Hanseatic League, is now Germany's most important Baltic port.

Altefähr
With its clear, uncluttered lines, this simple village church is a remarkable example of North German Gothic architecture. Built in the second half of the 15th century, the church is still the main focus of everyday life in the village.

Eldena Abbey
This ruined abbey was founded by Cistercian monks in 1199. From the 18th century onwards, it fell into decay and took on the appearance of Romantic dereliction which inspired the artist Caspar David Friedrich (1774-1840) to use it as a motif in a series of highly atmospheric paintings.

Ahrenshoop
The whitewashed fishermen's cottages, with their elongated thatched roofs, are let out to holiday-makers in the summer months; the accommodation is comfortable and reasonably priced.

St. George's Church in Wismar
A reminder of the senselessness of war: the late Gothic brick church was severely damaged by bombing in 1945 but is scheduled for restoration. The rest of the historic town centre has already been rebuilt.

**Chalk cliffs
on the island of Rügen**
With a sheer drop to the sea of over 100 metres, the chalk cliffs at Stubbenkammer were immortalized by Caspar David Friedrich.

Market square in Wismar
(Left) the "Alter Schwede", Wismar's oldest house, a merchant's residence built in 1380 or thereabouts and converted into a restaurant 100 years ago. In the foreground: the "Wasserkunst", a twelve-sided Renaissance pavilion with a domed copper roof which was the town's main well until the turn of the century.

else. Nobody in the small town is rich, and hence there is little envy. The members of the local élite congregate in a clubhouse, furnished in a comparatively elegant style, where wine and decent coffee are available, in addition to the usual beer. The club used to be known as the *Volkshaus* (People's House); after 1933 it was called the *Braunes Haus* (Brown House); subsequently it was rechristened *Haus der Gewerkschaften* (Trade Union House); today it once more bears the name *Volkshaus*.

A provincial idyll? Provincial maybe, but there is nothing idyllic about this busy, dirty industrial region. Saxony was to the GDR what North Rhine-Westphalia was to the FRG. One has the impression that the question who holds the reins of power in Berlin – capitalists, Fascists or Communists – is of little consequence to the small town. This may be disappointing to ideologues, but there is a good deal of truth in it. However, let us try to examine our observations a little more closely.

Many things have in fact changed. But coming from West Germany, the things one notices most are those which have remained intact. This probably has a good deal to do with human nature, but it is also determined by the particular situation of the GDR and by a further phenomenon which strikes me as characteristically "German" and which I find moderately intriguing.

The outside observer sees what people do, not what they think. Even in conversation, when strangers are present, the townspeople reveal more about their actions than their thoughts. However, the patterns of behaviour which one finds are dictated by experiences and pressures which are less dependent on political systems than ideologues are willing to acknowledge. These experiences are formulated in proverbs and scraps of German folk wisdom. The behaviour of these small-town folk, no matter whether they are ordinary citizens or Communists, appears to be guided by a set of *idées reçues* which includes the following maxims:

If you don't help yourself, nobody else will. Don't give yourself airs. The people in Leipzig think they know it all, but they haven't got a clue. The Berliners think they know it all, but they're a long way away. Thirst is worse than homesickness. It's all right as long as the cash comes in. Money makes the world go round. The eleventh commandment: don't let yourself get caught. You have to put the boat out now and again. There's no place like home. Keep your head well below the parapet. The worst thing of all is toothache. To be German is to do a thing for its own sake. Do as you would be done by. Somebody always gets left holding the baby. A bird in the hand is worth two in the bush. You have to cut your coat according to your cloth. I wish I had my time all over again. Who knows what comes after death. As you make your bed so you must lie on it. As the question so the answer. Do a good deed every day. Life must go on. It's all right for them at the top. We're all poor wretches really. – Of course the citizens of this small town in Saxony are very far from being the only people whose behaviour is governed by such maxims. The list is by no means complete, and not all the sayings are strictly applicable. But taken as a whole, they result in an astonishing continuity of human behaviour in a world of seemingly rapid change.

To Western eyes, the small town in Saxony appeared unchanged precisely because the Federal Republic had changed so drastically. European civilization follows a kind of law stipulating that major influences originate in the west and move eastwards. In his *Portrait of Europe*, published in 1952, the Spanish historian Salvador de Madariaga wrote: "Along the east-west European axis from Moscow via Berlin to Paris, one finds two sets of tensions: on the one hand there is the line of attraction, respect and imitation which runs from east to west, from Russia through Germany to France, and on the other there is the line comprising feelings of superiority, curiosity, deference and fear which runs from west to east, from France through Germany to Russia."

Left: The little boy is dressed in sailor's uniform, while his sister cradles her doll. As late as the turn-of-the-century, gender roles were rigidly fixed (ca 1900).

Right: This picture of two studious children with their governess was taken by the Württemberg court photographer Ludwig Holl. Education was still a privilege reserved for the well-to-do (ca 1905).

America can also be seen as part of this east-west axis. After the Second World War, a wave of Americanization swept through the world from west to east. It produced visible changes even in countries with stable cultures, such as France or England, and completely upset the inherently weak structures of the Federal Republic. But it stopped at the Iron Curtain. Although the east imported jazz and blue jeans and nylon shirts, and the west adopted vodka and caviar, this cultural exchange was strictly limited. The west has never been significantly influenced by the east. Ever since the emergence of the sovereign nation-states, the Russians have taken their lead from the Germans, who in turn have followed France and Britain; latterly, the French and the British have tended to model themselves on the Americans. Just as America has seldom emulated Britain or France, the French and the British have rarely imitated the Germans or the Germans copied the Russians.

Although Soviet promptings played a vital part in the rapid transformation of East Germany into a Communist state, the influence of the east on the GDR was less than that of the west on the Federal Republic. This is why, in the erstwhile GDR, the attribute which, for lack of a better word, we may call "Germanness", has been preserved in a far more pristine state. Admittedly, this is more the case in our small town in Saxony than in the GDR as a whole, where the huge state-owned steel combines, the collective farms and the monumental neo-classical architecture – to mention but three of the visible changes – do indeed represent something entirely new and unprecedented.

At this point the reader is bound to think, if he

Much store was set by regional loyalty and tradition. Arranged like a row of organ pipes, these three little boys proudly display their regional costumes (1911).

has not already done so, of this or that town in West Germany which has also remained more or less unchanged: either of those towns such as Rothenburg ob der Tauber which have been carefully preserved as living museums, or of the old Hanseatic cities which are firmly rooted in a constantly renewed tradition.

The reason why the small town in Saxony has changed so little is not only that its patterns of human behaviour, which are typical of small-town life, have remained astonishingly stable, or that the GDR was never "russified" in the same way that the Federal Republic was "americanized". When all is said and done, the principal reason is that the small town in Saxony is just that: a small town.

The Example of Beilstein

Although Germany has continually had problems with its national identity, it has also always had certain collective structures with a clear-cut and almost unshakeable conception of themselves. Not every German city is an identifiable unit in this sense, but many towns and villages do have a very definite sense of identity.

Take Beilstein, for example. Few readers are likely to have heard of Beilstein, so I shall explain a little about the place. In the year 1309, Kaiser Heinrich VII granted a charter to one Johann von Braunshorn, conferring the status of town on the houses at the foot of his castle, together with permission for ten Jews to settle there. The "town" never had more than 200 inhabitants; hence it remained a village,

In the Plain

The port of Hamburg
Two thirds of the port of Hamburg were destroyed in the Second World War, but it has now regained its place as the centre of maritime cargo traffic in Germany.

Hamburg
Free Hanseatic town and city state, with an evening view of the Binnenalster, which flows through the centre of the city.

Altes Land
The area of river-marsh on the west bank of the Elbe between Harburg and Stade is most notable for its pretty villages with orchards and neat rows of small houses.

Stade on the Schwinge
A mere village in Carolingian times, Stade is now a town, important for its Elbe ferry. The fine town houses testify to the municipal pride of this regional capital in Lower Saxony.

Lüneburg Heath near Schneverdingen
A typical view of the Northern German Plain between the Aller and the Elbe; the flocks of moorland sheep and the swarms of bees have almost disappeared.

Lüneburg
Impressions of the only fully-preserved example of the typical North German Gothic brick style.

The Tollensesee near Neubrandenburg
In the light of the evening sun, the lakeland landscape takes on a strangely archaic charm.

Windmill near Woldegk
For many hundreds of years, the strong winds of the north German plain have been used as a source of natural energy.

earning its living from the surrounding farms and the vineyards, which seldom produced a fully-matured wine. The castle passed into the hands of the Metternich family and fell into decay as early as the seventeenth century; however, Prince Metternich, the notorious Austrian foreign minister and opponent of Napoleon, still held the title Lord of Beilstein. And even today, the ruins of the fortress are known as "Beilstein Castle".

The "town" has scarcely changed since the early nineteenth century. The old church has become a community hall, the tithe-barn has been turned into a storehouse, and the Carmelite convent and the official residence of the Metternich estate manager have been converted into hotels. The main street is not in fact a street but a stairway which leads up from the market square – the smallest in Germany – to the Carmelite church above the Moselle valley. The church, like so many Catholic churches, is dedicated to the Virgin Mary, but in this case the Madonna is black, which is a considerable rarity. Parallel to the stairway, to the left and right, two so-called roads, which are no more than glorified dirt tracks, climb up into the Hunsruck hills. Along the bank of the Moselle there is a well-made country road which comes from Cochem, bypasses Beilstein and crosses the river at Senheim. Speaking of Beilstein, a chronicler remarks: "Almost nothing has changed here since feudal times." As in the small town in Saxony.

Of course, some things have in fact changed. One of the town's elderly inhabitants even tells me that "everything is different from the way it used to be." What he means by this is that arable and dairy farming have ceased as a result of tourism. People who visit the Moselle region want to drink wine. So vineyards are planted where they are easy to look after but where the quality of the grapes is even poorer than on the Klosterberg, which itself cannot exactly claim to be one of the Moselle's top growing areas. The old man also means that the effects of industrialization are making themselves felt in Beilstein. The Moselle has been canalized. There are limits to the mechanization of wine-growing. Young people are going off to work in factories. The tourists nowadays arrive in buses and excursion boats, instead of walking down from the Eifel and the Hunsruck or paddling up the river in canoes. Virtually every second house is now a wine tavern. The castle was taken over by an entrepreneur who festooned it with fairylights, put up a wire fence and charged a fee for entrance. Then it was discovered by the moviemakers, and Beilstein became moderately well-known as a setting for romantic films about the Moselle region.

Technology and tourism have certainly left their mark on Beilstein, just as they have affected the small provincial town of Stratford-on-Avon or the fishing village of St Tropez. But in some ways, Beilstein has managed to retain its identity in an ever-changing world. One sign of this is my friend Wolf Lippmann. He was Jewish, a descendant of the ten Jews who had been granted the right to settle in Beilstein by Kaiser Heinrich VII in 1309. Many of his forebears are buried in the old Jewish cemetery up on the hill behind the castle. This is truly continuity, extending right through the Nazi period, which one would scarcely expect in Germany.

However, anyone who tries to foist theories about race on the people of the Moselle region would only make a fool of himself. For centuries on end, Celts, Franks, Romans and Jews, followed by Frenchmen and Germans, were thrown together in the melting-pot. And what other people think, in Trier, Koblenz or Berlin – especially in Berlin – is of no interest whatever to the villagers of the Moselle, unless they can see some advantage in it for themselves or it is something they cannot possibly get out of. Apart from all other considerations, persecuting the Jews in the Moselle would have been entirely nonsensical. They were winegrowers like everyone else; they led the same life as everyone else; they too went to church, or not, as the case might be; they

The stiffly formal attire of these two young confirmation candidates and the objects with which they are pictured symbolize their entry into the adult world (1900/10).

even looked like everyone else.

Thus my friend got through the Third Reich unscathed, escaping the attentions of officialdom. There was only one nasty incident, when a couple of SS men in plain-clothes paid a visit to his restaurant. They sat out on the veranda, from which a steep, narrow flight of steps leads down to the Moselle. After their third glass of wine the two men began to rail against the Führer, grumbling about the war, which would soon be lost. Whereupon my friend, a man with the strength of an ox, declared, "I'm not having anybody insulting the Führer round here," grabbed the pair of them and threw them down the steps. Following this, however, he retired to his vineyard until the arrival of the Americans and the French three weeks later.

Is There a German National Character?

The murder of millions of Jews is an indelible stain on the history of Germany: the country carries a burden of guilt which can never be assuaged. But the notion of a specifically German anti-Semitism is based on the false conception of a German national character. There is and can be no such thing, for there is no group of "Germans" with a sufficiently long common history. In the towns of Germany, the Jews were assimilated long before anywhere else. Nowhere were they treated with greater tolerance than in Prussia under Frederick the Great. Before they emigrated to America, their contribution to intellectual life, to art and science, was greater in Germany than in any other country. Jews had always been numbered among the most fervent German patriots. How-

The message on the reverse of this postcard to the sender's grandmother in Berlin reads: "A souvenir of my summer holiday in Beelitz in 1912, from your grandson Otto Mathias". Beelitz is near Potsdam.

ever, there was indeed anti-Semitism in Germany, stemming from a variety of causes: religious enmity, economic dependence, professional jealousy, or the search for a scapegoat, which is always directed at minorities, in whatever country. And there was also the anti-Semitism which was imposed from above. When the gangs of SA thugs carried out the pogrom of 9 and 10 November 1938, burning down synagogues and demolishing Jewish shops, ordinary people did not actually actually join in, but nor did they intervene.

Oswald Spengler, who said it was conceivable that "the German people have no character at all", nevertheless remarked on the Germans' "endless need to serve, to follow, to worship somebody or something, with dog-like devotion and blind credulity, dismissing all objections…In no other country can a 'cause', a leader, or even a caricature of such things, be so sure of attracting a slavishly devoted following. This is a secret source of tremendous power for those who know how to use it." These were truly prophetic words, written six years before Hitler seized power. But are they really true, in a rational rather than a prophetic sense?

If it is the pressure of destiny, of experience and suffering, which shapes the collective character, the question arises whether this pressure can operate selectively. In other words: is it possible that there may be German characteristics, German abilities, inclinations and vices which do not add up to or cannot be subsumed into a "national character"? It seems to me that this is indeed the case. There are certain phenomena – ranging from German obedience to German inwardness, from *furor teutonicus*

**The Lakelands
of Mecklenburg**

Castle Klink on Lake Müritz, the largest of the Mecklenburg lakes. The name "Müritz" derives from the Slavonic word "morcze", meaning "sea".

Güstrow
Large, small and tiny lakes create the magic to be found in Mecklenburg. Here, a view of a lake on the outskirts of Güstrow.

Near Roggow
There are over 600 lakes of varying sizes in Mecklenburg, covering a total area of around 850 square kilometres.

By Lake Müritz, known as the "blue heart of Mecklenburg", near Vipperow.

Lake Müritz with a total surface of 117 square kilometres, Lake Müritz is almost twice the size of Lake Schwerin, which covers 63 square kilometres.

Schwerin Castle stands on an island south east of the town centre. Built mainly in the 19th century, in a style which harks back to the French Renaissance, the castle is a monument to the hankering of the erstwhile Grand Dukes of Mecklenburg for grandeur and prestige.

New Market Square in Waren
The half-timbered building on the left is the historic "Löwenapotheke" (Lion's Dispensary). On the right one sees the Parish Church of St. Mary, with its helmet-shaped Baroque dome.

Waren on the North Shore of Lake Müritz
Surrounded by woods and lakes, the 700-year-old market town of Waren has become an important recreational centre.

Market square in Wismar

Güstrow Castle, one of northern Germany's finest Renaissance buildings, is the ancestral seat of the Dukes of Mecklenburg-Güstrow. From 1628 till 1630 it was used as a residence by Wallenstein, the commander of the armies of the Holy Roman Empire in the 30 Years War. On the left one sees the gatehouse.

**Güstrow:
Ernst Barlach Memorial** in the former Chapel of St. Gertrude, with numerous sculptures by the artist, who died in Güstrow in 1938. A copy of his famous bronze sculpture "The Hovering Man" can be seen in the north hall of the Cathedral.

to the most recent forms of extremism – for which there is no other explanation.

Germany has always been marked by chaos and disorder. This is the country where the Teutonic tribes clashed with the Romans, where the interests of the great European dynasties conflicted, where the medieval Church broke asunder, where the middle-class revolutionaries of the west and the proletarian revolution of the east shook society to its very foundations, where in Roman times the *limes* cordoned off the north from the south and more recently the wall stood as a barrier between east and west. And where chaos reigns, there naturally arises a longing for order. It is a matter of historical coincidence that we refer to this country as "Germany", a highly flexible concept which is impossible to define with any clarity.

This country, which lies in the centre of Europe and has no clear-cut natural borders to the north and south, and whose western and eastern frontiers are even less definite, has often been urged to assume a role on the world-historical stage. "By its very situation, Germany is destined either to dominate the political life of Europe or to be dominated: there is no middle way..." This was the view of nationalists such as Julius Langbehn, writing in 1890. One can only hope that he will be proved wrong in the long run. Our aim must be to find the third way.

From the year 9 A.D. onwards, when the Teutonic tribes fought the Romans at the battle of Teutoburg Forest, there has never been a clearly definable German state or a nation with a distinct identity. All the attempts to create something of this kind have led, within fifty years at the outside, to excess and overweening ambition: they have then been either dropped or broken up by outside intervention. Compared with the dimensions of world history, the identifiable political units which have emerged from the ruins have been tiny, on a scale ranging between Beilstein and Bavaria.

Seen in the context of such world-historical upheavals, the things in Germany which have remained intact appear very small. The historical Germany may be a dream or a nightmare, demonic or contemptible, the world's public enemy number one or Europe's leading economic power; but the beautiful, the unchanging Germany is essentially provincial: a country of village inns, of towns with ancient gates and cathedrals, of rivers and hills. During the time that I have lived in Hamburg, I seem to have developed a certain civic pride in what I now see as a large, powerful and prosperous city. But I can still remember exactly how I felt when I arrived in Hamburg for the first time in 1954. Before then I had been living in London. And when I stepped out of the station and saw Mönckebergstrasse, Hamburg's equivalent of Regent Street or Oxford Street, it struck me as a small-town idyll. This is a small, beautiful country which from time to time has fits of megalomania, and then it is no longer beautiful.

Hamburg is not only a city, a proud former member of the Hanseatic League: it is also one of the ten *Länder* which made up the old Federal Republic. It belongs to the group of three *Länder* which have the least problems of identity. There is a second group, also comprising three *Länder*, whose identity is somewhat fragile; one of them is an ill-considered combination of two separate and clearly distinguishable units. And three of the *Länder* are purely artificial creations. Their lack of identity mirrors that of the former Federal Republic as a whole.

Next to Hamburg, the *Land* with the most intact sense of identity (despite the precarious state of the municipal finances) is Bremen. Like Hamburg, Bremen is a port, an old and traditionally cosmopolitan centre of trade with an unshakeable foundation. The third region with a definite identity is Bavaria, the biggest of the *Länder*, covering more than a quarter of West Germany. Bavaria has been in existence since 1180 and assumed its present form at the beginning of the nineteenth century. It remains a Bavarian mystery why this land should have survived the trials of German history in better shape than the other

Great importance was attached to maintaining the look of selfconfident composure seen in these two photographs of a student from Straubing, who is wearing the colours of his duelling society, and a young woman from Duisburg (1890/1910).

regions. In my view, it is largely a matter of chance, which cannot be explained away by any amount of supposedly profound reasoning. A particularly unconvincing explanation is the argument that Bavaria, as the most Catholic region of Germany, was also the most conservative of the *Länder* and put up the strongest resistance to change. This is controverted by the fact that, next to Bavaria, the most conservative Land is Schleswig-Holstein, a stronghold of Protestantism, which belongs to the group of regions with somewhat battered identities.

The Role of Religion in Germany

The seemingly naive use of superlatives such as "the most Catholic" and "the most Protestant" calls for a brief digression on the role of religion in Germany. It is impossible to overestimate the significance of religion in the country's history. Looking at the past, one's impression is of a mess of chaotic relationships between continually changing groups, clashing with each other or contriving to coexist and work together. This impression is now firmly established, but perhaps its real roots are to be found in the religious conflicts of the Thirty Years War rather than in the more remote past. After the Thirty Years War, peace never returned.

It is far more difficult to assess the part which religion plays in Germany today. Many observers claim that its role is defunct, but this is an oversimplified view. However, pictures of German churches and cathedrals are also deceptive. To infer from them that Germany is a fervently religious country would be just

It is uncertain whether this anonymous photograph was taken in a school classroom or a university lecture-hall. The young men are evidently waiting for their professor to arrive: some of them appear tense, while others wear a relaxed, nonchalant expression (1911).

as absurd as taking our wealth of fortresses and castles as an indicator of our military potential.

There are marked differences between the east and north of Germany on the one hand, and the south, below the River Main, on the other. The east and north have been shaped by Protestantism, whereas the south is predominantly Catholic. However, looking at the map, one soon realizes that this division is only an approximation: in the north we find the Rhineland, the Emsland and the Münsterland, which are solidly Catholic areas, and in the south there is Württemberg, the home of Pietism and the great Protestant thinkers.

Saying grace before meals and going to church on Sunday have become rare occurrences in Germany. However, most people still have their children baptised and confirmed, and give their parents a Christian burial; three in four of the population more or less uncomplainingly pay the relatively high church tax which is collected by the state and deducted at source, and from which people could easily opt out by leaving the church. It is often said that all this no longer has anything to do with religious belief; it is merely a desperate attempt to keep up tradition, or to retain a kind of insurance policy for the afterlife. There is a good deal of truth in this. But the question still remains why even people who consider themselves "progressive" cling to these time-honoured rituals. Why is it that they regard religion as an insurance policy? These are questions to which the churches have no answer: I myself have often posed them to clergymen. The churches are empty of worshippers, but in the summer months, the prettier ones are full of tourists, some of whom light consecrated candles:

**Berlin,
Brandenburg and
the Spree Forest**

Kaiser-Wilhelm Memorial church, Berlin
by night with the "Europa Center" in the background.

Charlottenburg Castle, Berlin
Originally known as the Lietzenburg Castle, it was renamed in 1705. Faithfully restored using old plans, it is now in service as museum.

Panoramic view of Berlin
To the left of the television tower one can see Berlin Cathedral. The modern building in front of the tower is the Palace of the Republic, whose façade is partly obscured by the Friedrich Werder Church. The domed roof on the left belongs to the Cathedral of St. Hedwig. In the background on the right one sees the skyscrapers on Karl-Marx-Allee.

Chinese Tea-House, Potsdam
Built between 1754 and 1757 by J. G. Büring, this tea-house in the grounds of Sanssouci Palace is a fine example of the 18th-century vogue for chinoiserie.

Chinese Tea-House, Potsdam
The base of the tea-house is decorated with gilded figures showing scenes of life in China.

Sanssouci Palace, Potsdam
Shortly after the laying of the foundation stone on 14 April 1745, the architect, G. W. von Knobelsdorff, fell out with his employer, Frederick the Great. Nevertheless, Sanssouci was to become one of Germany's most beautiful palaces.

Gardens of Sanssouci Palace, Potsdam
One of the most attractive German Rococo gardens. In the background, behind the terraced vineyard, one can see the palace.

Nikolaiviertel, Berlin
Between the River Spree and the Town Hall, the Nikolaiviertel is a recently-built replica of one of the city's historic quarters. Although it integrates a number of genuinely old buildings, its authenticity is somewhat doubtful. Nevertheless, it has a definite atmospheric quality. In the background one can see the television tower and the twin spires of St. Nicholas's Church, and on the left, the Cathedral.

Lehde in the Spree Forest

The Spree Forest to the north-west of Cottbus covers an area 75 kilometres long and 15 kilometres wide. The inhabitants, descendants of the original Slav population, are known as Sorbs. They have managed to preserve their traditional language and culture.

Lehde in the Spree Forest
The inland waterways known as "Fliesse" are the principal means of transport in the area. The houses are built on the so-called "Kaupen" (islands) between the canals.

Lübbenau: the gateway to the Spree Forest
The forest attracts over a million tourists every year. For most visitors, a punt trip along the unique canals is an absolute must.

A day out in the country
When there is something to celebrate, a trip through the countryside in a horse-drawn cart is still a popular treat.

one wonders if they do this out of curiosity or as a precautionary measure. In religious education lessons at German schools there is more talk of Buddhism and anti-authoritarian ideas about education than of the Father, Son and Holy Ghost. However, nearly all schools also offer Christian religious instruction, and these classes are well-attended.

The religious feelings of the Germans are probably neither stronger nor weaker than those of any other people. However, whereas in countries such as Italy, Spain, Britain and Scandinavia, a single unified religion helped to shape national identity, in Germany religion had quite the reverse effect: the antagonism between German Catholics and German Protestants was just as irreconcilable as that between German Communists and German liberals. Today, these religious differences are no longer irreconcilable. Yet the consequences of the Reformation, the Counter-Reformation and the Thirty Years War can still be felt.

Since the churches, in the plural, were unable to play any part in integrating the country, they were of no use to the thinkers and doers, the intellectuals and politicians. For anyone in Germany who wanted to achieve anything in this world, rather than the next, there was no point in turning to a religion which was split into two camps, both of whose support he needed. Hence religion and the churches lost their significance as a factor in the integration of society. They have remained as a source of spiritual consolation to those who need it; especially in the east, they remained as the only sphere of freedom in an all-powerful state; they have remained as the upholders of a past culture; they have remained as institutions which often achieve admirable things in the field of charity; they have remained as an ornament and an alibi in a state which is constitutionally committed to pluralism.

In Protestant Prussia, as in Catholic Bavaria, the church succeeded in maintaining its position, defined by the phrase "throne and altar", although this notion had already been largely undermined by 1918, when it was swept away by war and revolution. Something which has remained from all this, however, is the tendency of the south German *Länder* to orientate themselves towards France and the Mediterranean countries, whereas the northern regions take their cue from England and Scandinavia and the East Germans look to eastern Europe and Russia. In Munich, one is already half-way to Rome; if one travels to Hamburg, one is half in London; Frankfurt an der Oder is a jumping-off point for Warsaw and Moscow.

The German Länder: From Schleswig-Holstein to Bavaria, from Mecklenburg to Saxony-Anhalt

Schleswig-Holstein belongs to the staunchly Protestant north; its southern border runs through the city of Hamburg. Founded in 1460 by Christian I, who proclaimed that it would remain "up ewig ungedeelt" ("forever united"), Schleswig-Holstein suffered a certain amount of damage to its identity when it was "liberated" by Prussia in 1864 and annexed two years later: thus it became a Prussian province. Subsequently, Schleswig-Holstein swallowed up the old Hanseatic town of Lübeck, an erratic but homogenous block which was far from easy to digest. The people of Lübeck, proud of their town, still find it difficult to acknowledge Kiel as the regional capital.

Hamburg citizens see Schleswig-Holstein as the northern suburbs of Hamburg plus the coastal holiday area. Similarly, Lower Saxony could be described as the south of Hamburg plus the recreation areas of the Harz mountains and Lüneburg Heath. The Lower Saxons have even more justification than the Schleswig-Holsteiners for objecting to such a description. After all, they have to provide the inhabitants of Hanover, one of the largest German cities, with space to sleep and go about their leisure activities.

In this idyllic scene, time appears to stand still. The two old people have an air of complete serenity: they appear unperturbed by the bustle and rush of an increasingly hectic world (ca 1910).

This is the pattern which has emerged in the larger German cities as a result of rapid technical progress and commercial growth. The cities attracted workers from the surrounding region and from other parts of the country. Their population grew, and with it, the price of land and housing. Ordinary people were unable to compete with big companies which needed office space in the city centres, and they were driven out to the edge of town and beyond. Thus dormitory suburbs grew up around the periphery of the big cities. At the same time, the volume of traffic increased, the air pollution became worse and worse, and the noise and bustle became ever more unbearable: consequently there was a growing need to escape from the city at weekends or on free afternoons. The city-dwellers went out to look for recreation space and found it in the areas where there was little or no industry – such as the western part of Lower Saxony.

As far as the eastern part of Lower Saxony is concerned, the only place most people have heard of is the so-called Free Republic of Wendland which was founded by anti-nuclear protesters and subsequently depopulated by the police. East Friesia and the Emsland have remained undiscovered. Their gaunt beauty, with lakes, moors, heaths and mixed woodlands which grow sparsely on waterlogged ground, is unlikely to appeal to anyone whose notion of what constitutes a beautiful landscape has been shaped by holidays in the Mediterranean. I have found that only one German in ten from outside the region is capable of naming three or more towns in east Lower Saxony. And the first time most people heard of East Friesia was when they were told that

A year before the outbreak of war. The picture on the left shows an elderly lady from Würzburg with her grandson; the father and daughter on the right are from Brunswick. The figures are arranged in the usual stiff studio poses (1913).

the girls there wear headscarves to distinguish them from the cows – the East Friesians have replaced the Saxons as the butt of German humour.

The *Land* which is now called Lower Saxony is made up of four erstwhile feudal states: the Kingdom of Hanover, the Grand Duchy of Oldenburg, the Duchy of Brunswick and the Principality of Schaumburg-Lippe, all of which – like Schleswig-Holstein – were annexed by Prussia in 1866. Lower Saxony came into being in 1946: up to then, there was no region of that name. However, there was the tradition of the Guelphs, the former rulers of Brunswick and Hanover. This tradition was revived in order to give the inhabitants of Lower Saxony a new regional awareness.

The third and final member of this group of *Länder* with somewhat battered identities is Hesse, which first came into being as early as the sixteenth century, under the rule of Duke Philip the Generous. At that time, its borders were almost identical with those of the present *Land*, the only difference being that the administrative district of Montabaur was lost by a fluke of occupation geography at the end of the Second World War. Montabaur happened to be in the French-occupied zone, but it had been agreed that Hesse should be part of the American zone. Following a general law of inertia, things have stayed that way, although the occupying powers have long since removed the obstacles to a reorganization of the West German *Länder*, a possibility which is expressly provided for in the constitution. However, the sense of regional pride in the Länder is not really all that strong: at any rate, there has been no attempt by St. Goarshausen, Unterlahn, Unterwesterwald and

The Hercynian Mountains

Landolfshausen in the Weserbergland
Spa guests are attracted by the numerous springs in the rural Weserbergland between Minden and Münden.

Göttingen
View of the square in front of the Town Hall of this university town, with St. John's church and the famous Gänseliesel fountain.

Imperial Palace, Goslar
This market town on the edge of the Harz prospered thanks to silver mining in the Middle Ages and was a favourite residence of the Salian Emperors. The Imperial Diet met here on many occasions well into the 13th century.

Near Thale in the Harz Mountains
These rocks above the romantic Bode valley are wreathed in myth and legend. In prehistoric times they were the centre of a primitive cult.

Herzberg Castle, Harz
Following a fire in the 16th century the castle was rebuilt with magnificent half-timbering.
A striking example of German Renaissance architecture, this castle of the Guelph dynasty attracts many visitors to Herzberg.

Wernigerode
This medieval town, with its half-timbered houses, is situated on the northern edge of the Harz Mountains. The castle on the hill to the right, towering 350 metres above the town, was built in the 19th century on the site of an old fortress.

**Wahmbeck
in the Weserbergland**
Picturesque river-bank scenery moulded by the Weser and enlivened by a string of villages and small towns.

Wilhelmshöhe Castle, Kassel
Wilhelmshöhe Castle, formerly the residence of the Electors of Hesse, has one of the finest castle parks in Europe, with waterfalls and grottoes.

Saint Michael's Chapel in Fulda
The rotunda of the early 9th-century St. Michael's Chapel in Fulda cathedral is one of the earliest examples of Romanesque architecture in Germany.

Marburg an der Lahn
Documentary evidence of its status as a town goes back to the 12th century. In 1527 Marburg became the home of the first Protestant university in Germany.

Oberwesterwald, the Kreise which make up the Montabaur district, to found a "Back to Hesse" movement.

In south-west Germany, the geography of the occupation was corrected by a referendum on 8 December 1951. Because the Americans and the French wanted to keep their zones intact, the south-west had been divided up into three wholly artificial units: the *Länder* of Baden, Württemberg-Baden and Württemberg-Hohenzollern. They were amalgamated to create the *Land* of Baden-Württemberg. The hyphen cannot obscure the marked differences within the region, which may be ascribed to its geographical position or religion: Württemberg was quick to adopt Protestantism, whereas Baden, especially in the south, is Catholic. Although both the Kingdom of Württemberg and the Grand Duchy of Baden ultimately owed their existence to Napoleon, the people of Baden have always leaned more towards France than their neighbours. The Württembergers are said to be the most hard-working Germans; the Badeners, on the other hand, have the reputation of knowing how to enjoy life.

The antagonisms between the two halves of the *Land* are not sufficient to secure a democratic majority for the wish of many traditionally-minded Badeners to replace the hyphen between Baden and Württemberg with a definite line of demarcation. However, if you ask people in the region to define their identity, a citizen of Stuttgart will describe himself as a Württemberger or a Swabian, and a citizen of Freiburg will call himself a Badener. I have never heard anyone say, "I'm a Baden-Württemberger".

"I'm a North Rhine-Westphalian" or "I'm a Rhineland-Palatinater" would sound even more comical. These *Länder* are two of the post-war political creations which pose problems for the overall identity of the West Germans. North Rhine-Westphalia is the *Land* with the largest population and the least sense of a distinct identity. It was formed by the partial amalgamation of two Prussian provinces – Rhineland and Westphalia – which themselves were not readily identifiable units. The southern part of the Rhine province was then detached (hence the name "North Rhine"), and the old Principality of Lippe-Detmold was added to compensate for the loss. North Rhine-Westphalia is best defined in economic terms, as the Ruhr and its hinterland, which is how it was conceived by the British military administration.

At the southernmost tip of this hinterland lies Bonn, which became the Federal capital at the wish of Konrad Adenauer. We shall be looking at Bonn in more detail later. By incorporating the surrounding villages, it has grown into a small city with a population of over 300,000, but all further expansion is blocked by its geographical situation. The steep hills on either side of the Rhine mean that Bonn can only expand in a north-south direction, but to the north there is Cologne, West Germany's third-largest city, which is gradually creeping towards Bonn, and to the south, there is the regional border where North-Rhine Westphalia ends and Rhineland-Palatinate begins.

Rhineland-Palatinate is probably the most artificial of all the *Länder*. On August 30, 1946, the French military administration issued a proclamation amalgamating the southern part of the Rhine province with Hesse-Darmstadt, Hesse-Nassau and the Bavarian Palatinate. To make things even more complicated, a section of the Rhine province and part of the Bavarian Palatinate were then detached to form the Saarland, an autonomous region which was placed under the economic control of France in 1950.

A similar arrangement had been made in 1918. Lorraine and the Saar are natural partners: the one has iron ore and the other coal. So when the Germans won the war in 1871, they immediately annexed the whole of Alsace-Lorraine. When the French won the war in 1918 and 1954, they behaved in a more restrained fashion. They took over the Saarland, which was a much smaller area, but twice surrendered it again: the second time on January 1, 1957. But

The Burgtor in Dortmund (ca 1906). When the impending arrival of a train was signalled up the line, the gatekeeper at the level-crossing used to shout "Taumaken!" (a Low German dialect expression, meaning "Shut the gates!") to his assistants. Thus the crossing, between the northern part of the city and centre, became popularly known as the "Taumaker".

instead of being reassimilated into Rhineland-Palatinate, to which it had previously belonged, the Saar became a mini-*Land* in its own right.

The *Länder* of the erstwhile GDR, which have now rejoined the rest of Germany, follow the pattern which we have seen in the old Federal Republic. In the East, however, there are no wholly artificial administrative units of the kind found in the West, where instead of a single occupying power there were three allies, whose various interests had to be taken into account. On the other hand, the identities of the East German *Länder* have been somewhat weakened by the fact that for thirty-eight years they officially ceased to exist. In 1952 a programme of administrative reform was carried out, replacing the old *Länder* by districts known as *Bezirke*; the *Länder* disappeared from the map until 1990. But in the minds of their inhabitants, they were never completely abolished: Mecklenburgers never thought of themselves as "Bezirk-Neubrandenburgers", and no-one who lived in the *Bezirk* of Leipzig ceased being a Saxon.

Saxony and Mecklenburg are the two *Länder* whose sense of identity can be compared with that of Bavaria. But the identity of Brandenburg and Thuringia is no weaker than that of Schleswig-Holstein or Hesse. And even Saxony-Anhalt is less of a heterogenous and artificial creation than Rhineland-Palatinate or the Saar.

As inhabitants of a region which used to be an electoral principality and was elevated to the status of a kingdom by Napoleonic decree, the Saxons have retained more of their tribal character than the people of the other eastern *Länder*. It is no coinci-

Dortmund's Alter Markt is the centre of the city. In the "Restaurant zum Drachen", the half-timbered house mid-left, Dortmund democrats met at the end of the 19th century (ca 1906).

dence that the peaceful revolution of 1989 began in Leipzig and Dresden. The Saxons have never cared much for Berlin and its various governments. Allying itself with Austria and even with France, Saxony resisted Prussian expansionism for longer than any other part of Germany. Even after the foundation of the Second Empire, the Saxon lancers and riflemen remained loyal to their monarch, King Friedrich August III. Is all this now a thing of the past? The answer is no: wherever one looks, the past still continues to influence the present. When Walter Ulbricht, who came from Leipzig, ruled supreme in the GDR, people spoke of "Saxony's revenge on Prussia", and in Prussian East Berlin, the Saxons were referred to as "the fifth occupying power".

The people of Mecklenburg are very different from the Saxons, but they have an equally definite regional awareness. Compared with the brisk, bustling Saxons, they appear somewhat slow-witted and deliberate: as Bismarck is alleged to have said, they are a hundred years behind the times. They are a people of peasants and fishermen, who until 1918 were ruled by the landowning aristocracy. Although the Reformation separated Mecklenburg-Schwerin from Mecklenburg-Strelitz, which both acquired the status of grand duchies in 1815, the sense of belonging to a common tribe remained. However, the Pomeranians in the area west of the River Oder, which has remained German rather than being seceded to Poland, were seen as outsiders by the Mecklenburgers, despite what others see as the similarities between the two peoples. The University of Rostock in Mecklenburg has few complimentary things to say about the University of Greifswald in Lower Pome-

The Ruhr District and the Münsterland

Ahaus, Münsterland
Situated near the Dutch border on the north-western edge of the Münsterland, this district capital is surrounded by marshy land and heath.

Branch of the Dortmund-Ems Canal
The 267 kilometres of the Dortmund-Ems Canal link the eastern part of the Ruhr around Dortmund to Emden, thus giving the steel industry the convenience of a waterway to the sea.

Gelsenkirchen
"Town of a thousand fires", centre of iron and steel production and milling; also a centre of sheet glass and hollow-glass manufacture.

Gladbeck
A cross between industrial landscape and industrial monument. The old town centre is surrounded by extensive mining villages, with the occasional green space in between. Today more than half the pits are closed.

Dortmund
is the biggest city in the eastern part of the Ruhr. The recent economic changes in the region have had a positive effect on the city's external appearance. Apart from the Town Hall in Friedensplatz, Dortmund's main attractions are the opera, the theatre, the casino at Hohensyburg and the Westfalenhalle, which is the largest covered stadium in Europe.

Clemenswerth Hunting Lodge, Emsland
Situated in an area of extensive marshes and water-meadows, the lodge welcomed many a hunting party.

Nordkirchen Castle, Münsterland
Praised by contemporaries as the "Versailles of Westphalia", Nordkirchen Castle was built from 1688 to 1706 and was indeed modelled on the French original by its architect Pictorius.

Castle Burgsteinfurt, Münsterland

Intensive promotion of tourism is attracting more and more visitors to the delightful area between Vechte and Ems; it has a remarkable number of castles and stately homes situated on picturesque stretches of water.

Vischering Castle, Münsterland

Situated in the southern Münsterland, this is another example of a well-preserved fortress.

Münster Cathedral
Symbol of militant Catholicism in a Protestant region. Nearly seventy per cent of the inhabitants are Catholic, putting them in a comfortable majority; in the 16th century, however, the reformed Cathedral School was considered the "cradle of Humanism" in Northern Germany.

rania, which actually has a better academic reputation. But even with the millstone of Lower Pomerania around its neck – a very decorative millstone, it must be said – Mecklenburg is a region with a highly developed sense of individuality; its lakes and its extensive Baltic coastline also make it a region of soothing natural beauty.

The Brandenburgers, too, would have a strong regional tradition, extending way back into the past, had they not been taught to think of themselves as citizens of "Prussia", a name which was imported from the east. The Brandenburg of today is, so to speak, a chopped-down version of Prussia, which was pruned back to its original humble size by a decision of the Allied Control Council in February 1947. It is also the rural hinterland of Berlin, which both the Nazis and the Communists excluded from Prussia, whose capital was Potsdam.

Outsiders tend to underestimate the regional awareness of Thuringia, the extent to which the people of Weimar, Jena and Erfurt see themselves as Thuringians. Admittedly, this *Land*, too, is a mosaic, shaped by continual disputes over inheritance among the noble families of the region. It has always been a prize example of the fragmentation of Germany into a multitude of petty principalities: Saxony-Weimar-Eisenach, Saxony-Altenburg, Saxony-Coburg-Gotha, Saxony-Meiningen, Schwarzburg-Rudolstadt, Schwarzburg-Sonderhausen, the older and younger lines of the house of Reuss, and so forth. There is no denying the relationship with Saxony, but relatives often prefer to keep each other at arm's length. Whereas Saxony is a region of big cities – it includes Leipzig, Dresden and Chemnitz, the three largest cities in East Germany – Thuringia has more of a small-town character. In Saxony, the browns and greys of the industrial landscape are the predominant colours, but Thuringia, with the Saale valley, the Thuringian Forest and the Harz mountains, leaves a lasting impression of greenness. Thuringia is not a self-contained, enclosed *Land*, and it was easy to break the occasional piece off (Altenburg, for example) or tack the odd bit on (such as Erfurt). But if one views it as no more than a miscellaneous collection of small principalities, knowledgeable local inhabitants will point out that there was a kingdom of Thuringia as early as the fifth century.

Saxony-Anhalt is an altogether different case. As an East German *Land*, it remained in existence for a mere five years, from 1947 until 1952, when the *Länder* were dissolved. But the province first came into being in 1815, when it was taken away from the Saxons in consequence of their support for Napoleon. And the old Principality of Anhalt retained its independence from 1218 to 1945, although it was repeatedly divided and reunited. The "artificiality" of the region consists of the fact that it is an amalgam of two provinces which, like Baden and Württemberg, are closely linked by geography but have little historical connection with each other.

Saxony-Anhalt has been severely despoiled by the chemical industry. Hidden behind the grey-green clouds of poisonous fumes from Bitterfeld, Merseburg, Magdeburg and Halle lies one of the most charming valleys in Germany, the valley of the River Unstrut, which, after Meissen, is the country's northernmost wine-growing area. A part of the Harz mountains also belongs to Saxony-Anhalt.

The German *Länder* always have attracted a good deal of criticism, not only from convinced advocates of central government: in the ranks of the federalists there are also those who complain that as administrative units, the *Bundesländer* differ too much in size (the small *Länder* come in for particular criticism), and that they are too big and too heterogenous to create a genuine sense of regional community. In order to find homogenous entities which have more in common than a mere name, one would have to break up the big *Länder* such as Rhineland-Palatinate and North Rhine-Westphalia into smaller units. The Moselle valley or the Ruhr district, for example, are coherent areas which have been shaped by the same

Left: The Town Hall in Chemnitz, a town which expanded rapidly in the course of Germany's Industrial Revolution and became known as the "Saxon Manchester" (ca 1925).

Right: Magdeburg Cathedral, an imposing Gothic building whose tenth-century predecessor was destroyed by fire in 1209; work on the new Cathedral began immediately but was only completed in 1363 (ca 1920).

factors – the landscape, the weather, the economy – and where people share a common set of habits, fears and expectations. Nobody in the areas concerned remains unaffected by a poor wine harvest in the Moselle or a drop in the demand for coal in the Ruhr.

Hence the Saarland, Germany's most eccentric political creation, which came into being as the result of an annexation motivated by purely economic considerations, nevertheless has a certain character of its own, because it has a distinctive natural feature, one typical of the German landscape – a valley, or at least part of one. Coal and wine have shaped the destiny of the Saar, which is a thoroughfare between east and west, combining French cuisine with German refrigerators. When the government is German, the region is francophile; when the government is French, everybody loves the Germans. The inhabitants of the Saar valley refer to themselves as *Saarländer*, just as the *Moselländer*, the *Rheinländer*, the *Weserländer* and the *Emsländer* are happy to be known by the names of the valleys in which they live.

Organic Entities: The Towns

It must remain a mystery why there are no *Elbländer*, *Lahnländer* or *Innländer*. Perhaps the people from these valleys prefer, for whatever reason, to call themselves Hamburgers, Marburgers or Wasserburgers. Continuing our search for clearly definable units with a sense of identity, and taking a step further down the scale of size, we come to the city and the town, and eventually to the village or parish. Now that all the fishing villages have been turned

Halle an der Saale, a town whose prosperity was originally founded on the salt trade, is now the centre of the chemical industry in Saxony. It is also the birthplace of Georg Friedrich Händel; the house where he was born in 1685 is now a museum (ca 1900).

into seaside resorts and every last mountain village has become a winter playground, it has become almost impossible to find a German village community with an identity worth speaking of. At any rate, the villages no longer constitute a "totality of social relationships"; they have ceased to be "global societies on the basis of local unity", thus failing to meet the requirements of the sociologist René König for the smallest social system beyond the extended family.

However, many German cities and towns do satisfy König's requirements. They are the smallest and hence the most stable entities, the only units which can be clearly defined, unlike most of the *Länder* and quite unlike "Germany". Who can say where "Germany" lies (and where it ends) or what "North Rhine-Westphalian culture" is (the constitution guarantees the independence of the *Länder* in cultural and educational matters)? But there are few differences of opinion about a city such as Nuremberg and its contribution to German history; this is a subject on which it is easy to reach a consensus.

The Roman Empire helped the Germans to attain the level of civilization which is a prerequisite for founding cities. The first towns in Germany were built, directly or indirectly, by the Romans. Hence the oldest German towns are of Roman origin: Trier (*Augusta Treverorum*), Aachen (*Acquae Grani*), Cologne (*Colonia Agrippiensis*), Mainz (*Mogontiacum*), Regensburg (*Castra Regina*) and Augsburg (*Augusta Vindelicorum*). However, one should not think of these early towns as particularly urban places. They were fortified camps, built to house soldiers. Although the legionaries were soon followed by mer-

Saxony

Statue of Goethe and the Alte Börse, Leipzig
This monument to Goethe, who studied at Leipzig University, was erected at the turn of the century in front of the Alte Börse (1678-1687), the commodity exchange where the merchants used to meet to do business.

Wittenberg
A view of the market square. To the right, in the foreground, one sees the Renaissance Town Hall. The church in the background is the Castle Church, where Martin Luther initiated the Reformation in October 1517 by posting his 95 theses criticizing the system of Papal indulgences.

Bauhaus, Dessau
Designed by Walter Gropius and built in 1925/26, the Bauhaus occupies a central place in the history of modern architecture.

Castle Church, Wittenberg
This late Gothic church houses the tombs of Martin Luther and the great Renaissance humanist Philipp Melanchthon, who was Luther's most important collaborator.

Merseburg Cathedral
The oldest part of the cathedral, dating back to the early 11th century, is built in the Romanesque style. It was later extended to form a basilica with three naves and four towers. Among the many treasures in the cathedral archives is the manuscript of the "Merseburger Zaubersprüche". Written in the 10th century, this collection of pagan spells is one of the earliest documents of the German language.

Church of St. Nicholas, Leipzig
The church was founded in the 12th century. Between 1784 and 1797, the interior was redesigned by J. F. C. Dauthe and A. F. Oeser in a severe yet elegant classicist style.

Frankenhausen near Crimmitschau
A perfectly ordinary town in Saxony with factories, a housing estate and the inevitable football pitch.

Near Merseburg, a cathedral and county town on the River Saale. With a population of just under 50,000, it is dwarfed by the nearby cities of Halle (236,000) and Leipzig (555,000).

chants and artisans, these towns had no church, no town hall, no shops or streets in the conventional sense. All this came later, with the churches leading the way. The first cities founded by the Germans themselves, which date back approximately 1,000 years, were also fortified settlements, even if their purpose was only to guard a market or an important river crossing.

From the beginnings of Germany, which are shrouded in the mists of the Teutonic past, until well into the eighteenth century, it remained the case that where there was anything worth stealing, people had to fight to defend themselves against vagabonds, highwaymen, marauding soldiers, robber barons, jealous neighbours and hostile armies. Hence fortified walls and gates were essential features of the old German towns. They were followed by the town hall, taking charge of worldly affairs, and the church, attending to spiritual matters. These are the three basic elements of the German town (one also finds them in other European countries, but seldom outside Europe): the town hall, and later the guild-halls, which managed municipal business; the church, which oversaw the community's dealings with a higher authority; and the fortifications, which took care of the town's relationships with the outside world – a regrettable but characteristic aspect of life in those days.

In the course of time, the towns grew powerful, often more so than the Emperor and the temporal lords, but seldom as powerful as the spiritual lords, who commanded respect as agents of the higher mission without which bourgeois culture would have lost its *raison d'être*. Insofar as our culture remains bourgeois (*bürgerlich*), the credit for this must go to the German towns: the prototype of the *Bürger* is the citizen responsibly exercising his democratic rights in the town council. And the decline of bourgeois culture set in when worldly matters got the upper hand and the spiritual *raison d'être* withered away.

Today, for "aesthetic" or whatever reasons, many of us still admire these towns, with their three basic elements: the church, the *Rathaus* and the fortifications. Whenever Germany attempts to present itself in a positive light, the old towns are trotted out and shown, either *in natura* or in glossy coloured pictures, to the amazed foreigners. Over the centuries, their shape has changed considerably, but the features which constitute their basic character are still recognizable. The area which one may call "Germany" currently contains approximately 100 cities (it is difficult to name a precise figure, as new cities are constantly emerging). At the end of the eighteenth century there were only two cities of an appreciable size: Berlin and Hamburg. In the early nineteenth century they were joined by Dresden, and after 1850 by Leipzig, Cologne and Munich. During the first twenty years of the Wilhelmine Empire, the period known as the *Gründerzeit*, a number of cities sprang up which bore a certain resemblance to the cities of today. There were fifteen of them in all: Altona, Bremen, Hanover, Brunswick, Magdeburg, Halle, Chemnitz, Barmen, Elberfeld, Düsseldorf, Krefeld, Aaachen, Frankfurt, Nuremberg and Stuttgart.

Looking more closely at the history of the German towns, one realizes that a statement such as "Trier is 2,000 years old" feigns an identity which is entirely superficial. In respect of the past, it is impossible to speak of Trier as a "town" in the modern sense: until well into the nineteenth century, its population was under 10,000. Of the other towns founded by the Romans, only Cologne, Regensburg and Augsburg had reached the 10,000 population mark by the beginning of the sixteenth century; they were joined by Aachen in the seventeenth and Mainz in the eighteenth century. Before the year 1500, there was a total of a mere fifteen places in "Germany" which could be described as towns, taking a population of 10,000 or more as the yardstick: Lübeck, Rostock, Hamburg, Brunswick, Magdeburg, Halle, Berlin, Erfurt, Soest, Cologne, Frankfurt, Nuremberg, Regensburg, Augsburg and Ulm.

Since then, the cities and towns have grown immensely. In the process, they have lost part of their sense of identity, which is only to be expected, since expansion inevitably entails taking in heterogenous elements. They have also lost much of the power which their prosperity gave them in the past. Compared with the small principalities and dukedoms, the cities were wealthy, and this enabled them to buy their freedom from the ever-changing feudal potentates. Up until the end of the eighteenth century there were some fifty of these "free" cities, under the immediate aegis of the Holy Roman Empire. But when Napoleon dissolved the Empire, most of the free cities were "mediatized". Only six of them remained: Frankfurt, Nuremberg and Stuttgart, and the Hanseatic cities of Hamburg, Bremen and Lübeck.

Towns with Damaged Identities

Part of the legacy of this Golden Age of the German towns – golden in both senses of the word – is the financial benefit which the towns and the smaller communities still derive from the wealth and industry of their inhabitants. The taxes on property and trade go straight to the municipal authorities. But meanwhile, all kinds of new taxes have been invented: income tax, value-added tax and various indirect taxes on consumption. These taxes, which are forever going up, are collected by the central authorities: the Empire, the Federal government or the *Länder*. The proceeds add up to a sum which there is no point in naming, as it changes from year to year. But the key governing its distribution remains more or less constant. The Federal authorities take well over half the revenue from taxation, the *Länder* get a third, and the countless towns, villages and other communities share the remaining sixth. The German towns, which were once so rich, have now become poor.

The population of the towns has swelled, as more and more people come in from outside, not only from other parts of Germany but also from abroad. The towns have expanded massively as a result of industrialization; they have been deprived of their political power; they have been destroyed, in some cases several times over, by fire and successive wars. Despite all this, in the approximate area which we customarily call "Germany", it is above all the towns and the urban communities which have a definable identity, a distinct individual character. This is seldom to be found in the *Länder*; otherwise, apart from the towns, it is restricted to certain country districts. By no means all the towns have a clear identity, but the list of the ones that do would cover several pages. It makes more sense and is more instructive to take a look at the towns which have lost their identity or which never acquired one in the first place. It seems to me that there are four ways in which either of these things can happen: when attempts to build new towns fail; when urban conglomerations are created by building too many new towns in too small a space; when towns grow too quickly and incorporate too many heterogenous elements; and when towns or cities are divided. I shall endeavour to illustrate these four situations with four characteristic examples.

The official list of major German cities contains a place called Salzgitter. Other than on paper, this city is non-existent; it never has existed and it probably never will. The whole business is quite eerie. There used to be a small town known as Bad Salzgitter, and before the plan was hatched to blow it up into a city, it had a population of 3,000. It now has about 30,000 inhabitants. And it was turned into a city by counting in twenty-eight surrounding villages, some of which have since become small towns. Ten small towns and nineteen villages, not only with fields and woods and farmhouses, but also with huge steelworks, processing plants and ancillary services: all this became, or was supposed to become, the city of Salzgitter. The reason for this was that under the

continue p. 233

On 18 February 1921, the 350th anniversary of Luther's death, the Wittenberg Boys' Choir holds an open-air recital by the monument to the founder of Protestantism.

**Thuringia,
Dresden and the
River Elbe**

Castle Moritzburg near Dresden
Situated about 15 kilometres north-west of Dresden, this former hunting lodge and pleasure palace is now a Baroque museum.

Meissen
The old town of Meissen is dominated by the Cathedral and the Albrecht Fortress, which stand on a hill overlooking the town centre. In the foreground one sees the market square. Meissen is famed for its porcelain, which is exported all over the world.

Goethe's garden house, Weimar
A simple house in the park on the River Ilm, where the writer lived from 1776 to 1782. It was there that he wrote many of his nature poems and the first parts of "Iphigenie".

The Central Library of German Classical Literature, Weimar,
housed in the Green Castle.

The Wartburg Fortress in Eisenach is a collection of historic buildings of varying ages grouped around two courtyards; the oldest part of the fortress is said to date back to 1067. The Wartburg has always appealed to the German Romantic imagination.

The Ceremonial Hall in the Wartburg takes up the entire third floor of the fortress. The interior decor is from the 19th century.

The River Elbe near Dresden
A riverside panorama with Castle Albrechtsberg (left, 1851-1854), Castle Lingner (ca 1855) and the Tudor-style Castle Eckberg (right, 1859-1861).

Bastei in the Sächsische Schweiz
A labyrinth of ravines above the Elbe valley near Bad Schandau at the western edge of the "Saxon Alps".

The Royal Procession, Dresden
This long frieze depicting a royal procession was painted on the outer wall of the Castle between 1872 and 1876. In 1907 the picture was transferred onto porcelain tiles at the Royal Porcelain Manufactory in Meissen. The 93 figures in the procession include artists, scientists and members of the aristocracy.

Bastei in the Sächsische Schweiz
The Sächsische Schweiz is a paradise for mountaineers, offering over 5,000 different climbs. The view from the stone Bastei Bridge is a particular attraction for visitors.

Zwinger, Dresden
The Zwinger, a Baroque palace built by M.D. Pöppelmann between 1711 and 1730, is Dresden's best-known architectural monument.

Semper Opera House and Court Church, Dresden
The square in front of the Semper Opera House is gradually being restored to its former glory. The final step in the process of restoration will be the rebuilding of the Castle.

Zwinger, Dresden
This pavilion in the Zwinger synthesizes the architecture of M.D. Pöppelmann with the sculpture of B. Permoser.

From the Baltic to Bavaria,
from Cologne to Dresden

Literary Accounts of the German Regions

A Red Rock in the Sea

In the harbour towns along the coast one finds posters everywhere bearing the slogan "To Helgoland!", advertising the attractions of the island to tourists. Over the years, albeit at irregular intervals, I have been to Helgoland several times. Although it has no buildings of historical interest, the whole island is a kind of monument to the history of the earth. It is a natural monument, the remains of a mountain which sank into the sea in prehistoric times. Helgoland is a table of coloured sandstone which was once connected with the coast at the mouth of the Rhine, on the same latitude as northern Scotland. After hours of sitting on the ferry, it is always an experience to see the island gradually emerging from a grey desert of water: at first it is no more than a thin line on the horizon, but then it comes ever closer and grows into the symphony of colours described by the poet Hoffmann von Fallersleben: *Grün ist das Land / Rot ist die Kant / Weiss ist der Sand / Das sind die Farben von Helgoland.* (Green is the land / Red are the cliffs / White is the sand / These are the colours of Helgoland).

Hans-Heinrich Welchert

The Baltic Coast

Rostock. The main artery of this old Hanseatic town is the River Warnow, which is sufficiently broad and deep to accommodate a whole fleet of trading vessels, allowing them to sail right up to the warehouses, two miles inland from the mouth of the river. On winter days one finds some three hundred ships anchored in the heart of the town. Most of them come from Rostock itself, whose shipyards and shipping companies still have a high reputation in the towns of the Baltic coast. In the summer one sees a different picture. Most of the merchant ships are at sea; here and there the Danish flag or the Stars and Stripes flutters from one of the mastheads, but in general, trade appears to be at a standstill, although this is in fact the busiest season. The only ships out on the river are the steamers which ply between Rostock and Warnemünde.

Rostock is best viewed from the water, from its bulwark. As in all places which are laid out in this way, the riverbank and the houses along the quayside are the most picturesque part of the town. However, this area is far from elegant. One tavern follows another, and the signs and names over the doors are the best source of information about the places to which the ships of Rostock sail – names such as City of London and City of Falmouth, and above all the names of Swedish ports: Malmö, Kalmar and Wisby. Rostock does indeed do most of its trade with Sweden. Its relationship with the country dates back a very long way.

Warnemünde. Warnemünde is Rostock's sea port and also its Charlottenburg. The best way to travel there is by boat, on one of the river buses which are the main means of transport between the mother town and her daughter. One of these boats, a splendid old bird called *Phoenix*, takes us on her back and carries us down the Warnow. There is a slight drizzle, and a rainbow forms a bridge over the river.

Warnemünde, which has the reputation of being the Cinderella among bathing resorts, is actually not all that bad. There is no point in dwelling on the sins of the past and remembering the time when the town offered nothing but damp beds and flounder for dinner. This era has passed, and the flag of the North German League now flies on the towers of three hotels, above the heads of the just and the unjust, of Berliners and Rostockers alike.

Warnemünde has a distinctive architectural feature. Stuck onto the façade of each house, there is always a glass box variously called a balcony, a veranda or a pavilion. But whatever name people may give it, it is always the same box, on which the number of holidaymakers and hence the fate of Warnemünde both depend. Everything stands or falls with the glass box. These glass extensions give the place its particular character and contribute to the well-being of the guests. They are truly a boon...

Doberan. Right by the beach, no more than fifty yards from the window at which I sit and write, there is a granite block which informs the visitor, in gold lettering, that the Grand Duke Friedrich Franz founded the first-ever German bathing resort on this very spot in 1793...

The seaside resort of Doberan, as distinct from the town of the same name, half a mile inland, is situated directly by the sea, on the so-called *Heiliger Damm* (Holy Embankment)...

In the early decades of the present century, Doberan in the bathing season had a social life of which only the barest trace now remains. Doberan was the meeting-place of the Mecklenburg aristocracy, a kind of Round Table where the knights of the land congregated around their King Arthur. In this case the role of the king was played by Grand Duke Friedrich Franz...

The climax of these golden days was the season in Doberan. In the past, people did not stay on the Heiliger Damm but in the town itself. There were horse races, and performances by the court theatre and the court musicians; people played roulette and Pharaoh, and every day they drove to the beach and back again in splendid carriages, returning in the evenings to dine at the *Kurhaus*, which even then was already on the Heiliger Damm. The Grand Duke presided over the proceedings, and those present were in a sense his personal guests...But these days are now long past...

In its present form, the Heiliger Damm comprises a dozen lodging-houses down by the beach. The larger houses are built in a style which looks like a cross between a hotel and a castle; the small ones resemble English cottages. Here the descendants of the old barons sit in their cramped apartments which have no more than three or four rooms. Unless the keen northwesterly wind is blowing, the sea is boring, lapping back and forth in a gentle swell. Not a ship or a boat is to be seen. The holidaymakers read the newspaper, play billiards or whist and eat breakfast. Fortunately the latter business can be extended over a considerable period. The ladies bathe and sleep, prink and preen themselves four times a day, take the air in the marshy beech wood, which smells of leaf-mould, and occasionally run their fingers over the grand piano in the *Kursaal*, not actually playing the instrument but merely testing it...

The sea is calm, and life is quiet. The occasional wave breaks, but it is too small to interrupt the silence. The uninhibited gaiety of the old days has gone; the sea air has turned stagnant. A pall of leaden tedium hangs over Doberan...

Theodor Fontane

Rügen: Megaliths and Chalk Cliffs

Eroded on all sides by the sea, Rügen has the jagged shape of a vineleaf; projecting out from it, there are as many tongues of land as a sea spider has legs, and yet it is the Baltic's most charming island: our northern Arcadia.

The island owes much of its reputation as a beauty spot to the fact that it can only be approached by boat or from Pomerania, but it has natural attractions which are just as sublime as those of southern Germany, although they are less dramatic. The gigantic upheavals of nature, whose effects are so clearly apparent, and the monuments from the distant past fill the soul with a deep sense of awe. By monuments I mean the prehistoric burial sites covered with huge blocks of granite: in these graves, entire human skeletons have been found, sitting upright with their arms folded across their chests, surrounded by weapons, chains, rings and urns filled with ashes. The deeds and even the names of these prehistoric people are sunk in oblivion; trees now cover the oval burial mounds, and the idle curiosity of later generations has disturbed the bones and their resting-places: many of the urns have been destroyed, without a proper examination, by people eager to see what was inside. On seeing a fly trapped in a piece of amber, Kant once exclaimed: "If only you could talk, little creature, how much greater would our knowledge be!"

With the keenest expectations, which were not disappointed, I embarked on the half-hour journey by ferry from Stralsund, best viewed from the sea, to the enchanted island, where one sees both nature, in all its opulence, and the results of human industry...

We are at the edge of these famous chalk cliffs, which, to be sure, are not 600 feet high, but must be well over half this alleged figure, and at the foot of the precipice the sea surges and billows. The cliffs are almost entirely composed of chalk, mixed with flint, and when it rains, the sea in the surrounding area turns white.

The highest point of the cliffs is the so-called King's Seat, on which Karl XII is alleged to have sat: a test of daring which any Tyrolean mountain infantryman would pass. A footpath leads down to the shore, which is the best place from which to see the bizarre rock formations. At the top there is a grassy bank, shaded from the sun by a clump of beech trees. One is overwhelmed by a sense of infinity, a feeling which I shall not attempt to describe. In the absence of whitewashed walls, vain fools carve their names in the bark of the trees.

Karl Julius Weber

Hamburg

Hamburg!

It is more than a conglomeration of stones, roofs, windows, wallpaper, beds, roads, bridges and street-lamps. It is more than factory chimneys and the tooting of car horns, the laughter of the seagulls, the clattering of the trams and the thundering din of the railway; more than ships' sirens, screeching cranes, swearing and dance music – it is infinitely more than all these things.

It is our will to be. Not to be just anywhere or anyhow, but to be here and only here, between the Alster and the Elbe – to be as we are, we, the people of Hamburg. We unashamedly admit that the sea winds and the fog on the river have bewitched and beguiled us into staying here. That the Alster has seduced us into building our grand houses around it – and that the river, the broad grey river, has seduced us into following our hankering for the open seas, wandering far and wide, sailing away in order to return, diminished and weakened by homesickness, to the small blue lake amidst the green-helmeted towers and the greyish-red roofs.

The city of Hamburg: a stone forest of towers, street-lamps and six-storey houses, a forest whose floor is made up of paving stones which tap out a magical rhythm: at night, you can still occasionally hear the footsteps of the dead.

The city: a primitive animal, scuffling and snorting; an animal made up of courtyards and glass and sighings, of weeping, parks and screams of lust – a primitive animal whose eyes – the silvery, oily canals – glint in the sunlight. An animal whose eyes – the flickering street-lamps – glimmer in the moonlight.

The city: a home, a heaven, a haven; a mistress between heaven and hell, between two seas; a mother between meadows and mud flats, between dyke and river; an angel between sleeping and waking, between fog and wind: Hamburg!

Wolfgang Borchert

Worpswede

It is a strange land. If you stand on the little sandhill of Worpswede, you can see it spread out all around, like the peasants' kerchiefs with their dark centre and their corners showing flowers of a deep brilliance. It lies flat before you, with scarcely a fold, and the roads and water-courses lead far into the horizon. A sky begins there of indescribable variety and spaciousness. It is reflected in every leaf. Everything seems to be occupied with it; it is everywhere. And the sea is everywhere. The sea, that is no longer, that ebbed and flowed here thousands of years ago, whose dune was the sandhill on which Worpswede lies. These things cannot forget it. The great murmuring filling the old pines on the hill seems to be its murmur, and the wind, the mighty, sweeping wind, brings the smell of it. The sea is the story of this land. It has hardly any other past.

Once, when the sea withdrew, it began to take shape. Plants unknown to us appeared and there was quick and hasty growth in the rich layers of mud. But the sea always returned with its highest tides, to the regions it had left, as if it could not be separated from them, and in the end there remained black, boggy marshes full of watery creatures and slowly decaying fertility. The flats thus lay solitary, completely self-engrossed, for centuries. The heath was formed. And finally it began, at isolated spots, to close up as a wound closes. About this time, which is generally reckoned to be the thirteenth century, monasteries were founded in the Weser valley, which sent Dutch colonists into these districts, into a hard, uncertain life. Later there followed (at rare enough intervals) fresh attempts at colonization in the sixteenth century, in the seventeenth, but only in the eighteenth was there a definite plan, the energetic carrying out of which rendered the lands by the Weser, by the Hamme, Wümme and Wörpe, permanently inhabitable. Today they are fairly well populated. The early settlers, as far as they were able to persist, grew rich by the sale of the turf; their successors led a life of labour and poverty, close to the earth, as if under the compulsion of a stronger force of gravity. Something of the sadness and homelessness of their fathers lies upon them: their fathers, who left a life behind them when they went forth into the black, boggy land to begin a new life, knowing not how it would end. There is no family likeness among these people; the mothers' way of smiling is not passed on to the sons, because the mothers have never smiled. They all have but the one face: the hard, tense face of work, the skin of which has been stretched by all their labours so that in old age it is too large, as a much-worn glove is too large. One sees arms made disproportionately long by the lifting of heavy objects, and backs of women and old men grown crooked, like trees which have stood always in the same storm. The heart in these bodies is crushed and has not unfolded. The mind is freer and has developed in a certain one-sided way. No increase of depth, but a sharpening of it in inventiveness, maliciousness, quick-wittedness. Their language helps them there. This Low German (*Platt*) has a natural vitality in it, with its short, taut, colourful words, that move as if with atrophied wings and webbed feet like marshland birds. It is to the point and passes over easily into noisy clattering laughter, it learns from the occasion, it imitates sounds, but is not enriched from within outwards: it makes a beginning. It is heard often from afar during the midday rest, when the heavy labour of turf-cutting, compelling silence, is interrupted. It is rarely heard in the evening, when weariness comes early and sleep enters the houses almost with twilight.

Rainer Maria Rilke

Berlin

The huge city of Berlin which he had not visited for a long time made an enormous impression on him. He traversed the streets leading from the centre to the West End, Lennéstrasse, Hitzigstrasse, the Kurfürstendamm. He saw the never-ending stream of cars which rolled on with the matter-of-factness of a river, stopping temporarily only to roll on again. He noted the perfect working of the apparatus designed to control the stream of traffic, the automatic stopping signals, the islands in the middle, the traffic policemen, the light signals, yellow, red, yellow, green. He took an aimless ride on the Overhead and Underground railway, and was taken over

Germany in Old photographs, 1850-1920: From Bremen to Stralsund

Kiel
The town's banking quarter is situated on the "Little Kiel", a kind of lake formed by the broadening of the Kiel Fjord. Its upper reaches are now completely built over. This photo, taken in about 1900, shows the bridge over the "Little Kiel".

Hamburg
Still preserving its reputation as one of the finest promenades in Germany is the Jungfernstieg, with boats for hire and an old landing-place for steamers, photographed 1903 here before the construction of the monumental edifices designed by Fritz Schumacher.

Hamburg
View of Hamburg's harbour for sailing ships (ca 1904).

Bremen
Bremen, which stands on a stretch of dunes traversing the Bremen basin on the right bank of the Weser, was first mentioned in documents in 782 and developed rapidly as a ferry port and commercial centre. The photograph shows the view looking north (ca 1920).

Herrenhausen Castle, Hanover

The former residence of the House of Hanover was destroyed by bombs in 1943. This photo taken at the turn of the century shows the view of the castle from the gardens.

Hanover
Division of the river Leine
at the Hohes Ufer (ca 1900).

Schwerin
View from the Castle to the State Theatre (right) and the brick-built Gothic Cathedral (ca 1920).

Güstrow
The Horse Market with the Borwin Fountain. In the background one can see the tower of the Parish Church of St. Mary (pre-1895).

Rostock
The New Market (Ernst-Thälmann-Platz) and the Town Hall, a Gothic brick edifice with a Baroque façade (ca 1922).

Binz on the island of Rügen
Although mass tourism is a post-war phenomenon, the popularity of seaside holidays dates back to the turn of the century (1904).

Stralsund
The Town Hall on the Old Market is an exceptionally fine example of north German Gothic brick architecture (ca 1900).

that space in the middle of the city where countless tracks meet, where trains go shooting over and under, cutting across and overtaking each other. He emerged from the shafts of the Underground into some street or other, and saw houses and more houses, people and more people, endlessly going on. He walked through the long subterranean passage in the middle of the city which was filled with hurrying, busy people anxious to catch a connecting train at the other end. He noticed that the millions of inhabitants in this city did not stand gossiping at corners like his fellow-citizens at home, but went about their business hastily, coolly, and yet without self-importance. He observed the swarming working-class districts, the swaying motor-buses, the rows of shops. The enormous, gorgeously lit-up places of entertainment, cafés, cinemas and theatres, by tens, by thirties, by hundreds and thousands, all filled with people. Processions of the Right wing radicals under police escort, in sports jackets and caps, flourishing the Indian emblem of fertility on flags and placards, marching in fours, numerous enough. Processions of Left wing radicals with the emblem of the Proletarian Union of Russian Soviets, the six-pointed star, the sickle and the hammer, in endless numbers. He saw the roads leading out of the city towards the surrounding lakes, into the scanty woods filled with town houses, every road packed with people, cars and motor-buses. He was a man of facile enthusiasm, and he savoured appreciatively the manifold life of this populous city which was so sure of itself, enjoying its dimensions and the precise functioning of its organs.

Lion Feuchtwanger

A Walk in Potsdam

But now I think it is time for us to stroll over to the parks, if we are to see anything before it gets dark. Out here, between the Berlin gate and the Glienicke bridge, Potsdam becomes a military town with suburban elements; it loses its elegance and has only a handful of buildings which are worth looking at.

The transformation of the Bassinplatz into a square has surely impaired its character. The small building in the centre was once a tea-house of the kind popular in Holland; it was surrounded by water on all sides and provided a refuge from the heat on summer afternoons. Standing here, it now looks somewhat out of place. Every child in Potsdam will tell you that the famous Tobacco Club used to meet here at night, but scholars maintain that this is a legend.

On the far side of the square, which is now a kind of parade ground, one sees the Dutch Quarter, which must also have been jollier to look at when its appearance was reflected in the water.

But there are certain times when I rather like the square, for example when it is filled with the old-fashioned small-town charm of the Christmas market, which creates an atmosphere of colour and gaiety.

And you really must go to Wilhelmplatz down by the canal to see the fish market which, if my memory serves me aright, takes place in the afternoons under the tall trees by the iron railings designed by Manger. There the fishwives sit in a long row in front of their stalls, where the fish wriggle and splash. The women wear oilcloth hats and sit on little wooden seats which look like old-fashioned children's sledges. They remind one not so much of Zille or Hosemann but of Doerbeck's caricatures of typical Berlin figures, published in 1820. Even today, among these women, one could surely still find a granddaughter of the fishwife Frau Wulkow whose quiet, motherly tenderness enhanced the life of my young hero Heinrich Schön before destiny led him onto another, more dangerous path...

Charlottenstrasse has now become a shopping street, with plate-glass windows and obtrusive, shamelessly self-important shop signs; these things have ruined the overall effect which was once so charming. The long rows of shop fronts can be compared with a string of pearls, in which some of the pearls have been damaged and others have been replaced by poor-quality imitations. However, if one is prepared to ignore these, one is surprised by the number of real pearls which still remain. The buildings are richly variegated, with examples from nearly all the categories I have mentioned. Perhaps the finest of them are the houses designed by Unger, making attractive use of cherubs, vases and pilastres which divide up the façades. Was he perhaps the architect of the pair of semi-detached houses, numbers 86/87, in which the former senior civil servant Herr von Mühlensiefen, a character in one of my novels, eked out his meagre pension? Perhaps it was that house there, with the pretty balconies flanked by groups of cherubs: plump and gawky giant babies at play? *Chi lo sa* – this was before the time when balconies came into fashion. Where they existed at all, they were not designed for people to sit on; they were merely part of the architectural structure. Insofar as they had a purpose, it was to allow the inhabitants of the houses to step outside for a second, to receive public ovations, or to look briefly down into the street: otherwise, the mirror mounted by the window served as a means of observing the goings-on outside.

It would be interesting to know whether these window mirrors, which were known as "spies", were already in use in the Rococo period. I am still uncertain whether this was the case, despite the exhaustive research which I once carried out in Neustrelitz, the "spy" El Dorado.

Georg Hermann

Göttingen

The town of Göttingen, celebrated for its sausages and University, belongs to the King of Hanover, and contains nine hundred and ninety-nine dwellings, divers churches, a lying-in asylum, a prison, a library and a *Ratskeller* where the beer is excellent. The stream which flows by the town is called the Leine, and is used in summer for bathing, its waters being very cold and in more than one place so broad that Lüder was obliged to take quite a run before he could leap across. The town itself is beautiful, and pleases most when looked at backwards. It must be very ancient, for I well remember that five years ago, when I was matriculated (and shortly after "summoned") there, it already had the same grey, old-fashioned, wise look, and was fully furnished with droll stories, poodles, dissertations, *thés-dansants*, washerwomen, compendiums, roast pigeons, Guelphic orders, doctoral coaches, professors ordinary and extraordinary, pipe-heads, court-counsellors and law-counsellors and all kinds of other nonsense. Some people even maintain that at the time of the great migration of races, every German tribe left an uncorrected proof of its existence in the town, in the shape of one of its members, and that from these descended all the Vandals, Friesians, Swabians, Teutons, Saxons, Thuringians and others, who still abound in Göttingen, where, separately distinguished by the colour of their caps and pipe-tassels, they may be seen straying singly or in hordes along Weenderstrasse. They still fight their battles in the bloody arena of the Rasenmühle, the Ritschenkrug and the Bovden, still preserve the customs of their savage ancestors, and are still governed partly by their Duces, whom they call "chief cocks", and partly by their primevally ancient legal code, known as the *Comment*, which fully deserves a place among the *legibus barbarorum*.

The inhabitants of Göttingen are generally divided into students, professors, Philistines and cattle, and the distinctions between these estates are far from clear. The cattle class is the most important. I might be accused of prolixity if I were to enumerate all the names of the students and all the regular and irregular professors; besides, I do not at present quite remember all the students' names, while some of the professors as yet have no name at all. The Göttingen Philistines must be as numerous as the sands (or rather the mud) on the sea-shore; indeed, when I saw them of a morning, with their dirty faces and clean white bills, waiting at the gate of the University court of justice, I found it almost impossible to understand how God could ever have created such an innumerable pack of rascals.

Heinrich Heine

The Harz Mountains

Thus the Harz was the first and the most impressive range of wooded mountains I ever saw. The massive barrier of trees, part decidous and part conifer, combining black with variegated shades of green, has a striking visual impact, stemming from the way in which it suddenly rears up from the plain with no visible transition. At certain times of the year, there is something abrupt and vaguely threatening about the Harz; at all events, it is highly spectacular. It is what the experts call a horst, the remains of a vast plateau which in the Devonian age extended all the way to the North Sea. There is something artificial about the heavy, bulky humpback shape of the Upper Harz, which looks as though it had been stuck onto the flatter Lower Harz as an afterthought. To me, the character of these mountains is still largely determined by the Upper Harz area to the north and west, between Harzburg and Goslar on the one hand and St Andreasberg and Lautenthal on the other. As an adolescent I explored this area on foot: I walked through the Oker valley, for example, invariably setting out from Altenau and ending up in Goslar. It was a day's trek through a characteristic Upper Harz valley, one which is not particularly narrow but whose steep slopes and bare rocks nevertheless create a sense of confinement. The Romkerhalle waterfall half-way between Altenau and Goslar never ceased to amaze me. The relative narrowness of the valley at this point heightened the effect of the foaming curtain of water and gave it an impressive air of violence.

Even in those days, there was a fair number of other walkers on the mountain path which we took. To me, however, the route conveyed an impression of solitude and forlornness. Shortly after leaving Altenau, one came across the empty workings of an abandoned silver mine. All the way to Schulenberg and for some way beyond, the scene was the same: it seemed as if the countryside were waiting for something. The plan to build a dam across the Oker valley had not yet been put into effect. Today, the Oker reservoir extends northwards right up the valley. When it was built, a number of villages had to be abandoned and their inhabitants rehoused elsewhere. Among these sunken villages was Schulenberg, which was re-founded as Neu-Schulenberg.

The impressions of one's youth linger obstinately in the mind. When I think of the Harz, I see isolated details: the abandoned silver mine, the wall of black fir-trees, the trout-filled stream between Altenau and Clausthal, the piles of wood between the tiny houses whose shingle roofs extended right down to the ground, the feathers of the cock canaries, the goitres of the old women, the children´s coats called *Nennen* - things of the past which have vanished but are not forgotten. Life here was different. People cared little for the outside world, rarely marrying out of the area or moving elsewhere, even when the poverty was harsh. They

were simple and happy and showed an unexpected friendliness. I hear the sound of cowbells from invisible meadows...The Harz seemed to be inhabited by the ghosts of the past. With its dense pine forests, it was at once lonely and inviting, until tourism opened up the last corners of the area.
Karl Krolow

The Wartburg

At that time, the Wartburg had not yet been restored. It was quite a plain, undistinguished building: even the old house of the Landgraf, with its barn-like roof and its mainly walled-up windows, struck one as dull and austere, while the so-called New House, built during the reign of Karl August, was executed in the most "modern", paltry style. It contained the armoury, next to which there was a small guest-room with a single window; the big tower had yet to be built.

The most picturesque part was the gatehouse at the front, with the so-called Luther House. The big rooms above the gate, which was manned by a detachment of six guards, were used as a restaurant, whose proprietor lived in the rooms on the ground floor of the Luther House, immediately adjoining the gatehouse. One of these rooms was occupied by Arnswald's orderly, a man called Juch, whose services as a factotum we quickly came to appreciate, for he was always good-humoured and obliging. On the first floor of the Luther House there was Arnswald's charmingly furnished sitting room and next to it, his bedroom. The Luther Room was across the hall; it adjoined the rooms of the Grand Duke, which were seldom used, and unless the Duke had guests staying, which was a rare occurrence, these chambers, too, were at Arnswald's disposal.

However, the rooms normally reserved for guests were the attic rooms in the Luther House which had formerly served as a prison: from here, one had a delightful view of the Forest of Thuringia, the Hörsel Mountains and the valley of the River Hell, immediately below the castle. For many, many years I was a regular guest in these rooms, and the hours which I spent with Arnswald at the castle were among the most poetic and rewarding of my entire life.
Friedrich Preller the Younger

Weimar: Narrow Streets and Broad Horizons

I arrived at Weimar, where I regained my courage on seeing, through the difficulties of the language, the immense intellectual riches which existed outside France. I learned to read German, and I listened attentively to Goethe and Wieland, who, fortunately for me, both spoke French extremely well. I understood the mind and genius of Schiller, despite the difficulty he felt in expressing himself in a foreign language. The society of the Duke and Duchess of Weimar gave me great pleasure, and I spent three months there, during which time the study of German literature gave all the occupation to my mind which it requires to prevent me from being devoured by my own feelings.

Of all the German principalities, Weimar most clearly demonstrates the advantages offered by a small country whose monarch is a man of intellect and who endeavours to please his subjects while maintaining his authority...For the first time, Germany had a cultural capital, but one which at the same time remained a small town, and whose influence thus consisted solely in the light which it radiated; fashion, which always brings uniformity into everything, could scarcely take such a narrow circle as its starting-point...

When I stayed in small towns, I always found them very tedious. The minds of the men grow narrow and the hearts of the women become numbed; everybody lives in the constant society of the same set of people, so that one is oppressed by one's own kind. Things are no longer judged from a distance, in a way which animates the spirit and echoes from afar like the thundering commotion of fame; everything you do is carefully watched, every last detail is subjected to narrow-minded scrutiny, and this makes it impossible to grasp your character as a whole. The greater a person's urge for independence, the more difficult it becomes for him to breathe, in the face of all these petty constraints and restrictions.

This agonizing lack of freedom was not to be found in Weimar, which was not really a town at all: it was more like a big castle, where a select circle animatedly talked about all the latest developments in art. There were women, charming disciples of great men, who ceaselessly occupied themselves not only with works of literature but also with public affairs of the highest importance. Through reading and study, one communed with the universe, escaping the narrow bounds of circumstance by the breadth of one's mental horizons. Talking in society about the major questions which shape our common destiny, one forgot about the petty affairs of the individual. Here, one encountered not a single example of that species of provincial fops who confuse arrogance with refinement and affectation with elegance.
Anne Louise Germaine de Staël

Scenes from Westphalia

Gradually, however, the prospect becomes more welcoming: in the lowlands there are occasional patches of grass, and the clumps of trees become greener and more frequent, greeting us as the advance guard of the fertile lands beyond. Soon we find ourselves in the heart of the Münsterland, an area as charming as any place can be which completely lacks moun-

**Germany in
Old photographs,
1850-1930:
From Berlin to
Chemnitz**

Berlin
View of Berlin's Alexanderplatz as it was in about 1894. After the Second World War it was completely rebuilt.

Berlin
This panoramic view taken in about 1900 shows the Cathedral, St. Mary's Church and the royal castle, which as a symbol of the detested Prussia, was demolished by the Soviets in 1950.

Berlin
The Brandenburg Gate on Pariser Platz. An early example of the neoclassical style in Germany, it formerly symbolized the divided city (1895).

Frankfurt an der Oder
View from the Church of St. Mary to the river. The building in the foreground is the Town Hall (pre-1920).

The Spree Forest
Wearing traditional costume, the two Sorb girls punt the elegantly-dressed company through the canals of the Spree Forest (1913).

The Spree Forest
Even the postman uses a punt to do his rounds (1910).

Near Berlin
In the outdoor restaurants of turn-of-the-century Berlin, the well-to-do middle class rubbed shoulders with the poor: "Coffee-Making Facilities Available for Families" (1910).

Magdeburg
The Old Market, with the two-storey Town Hall (1691-1698) and the statue of the Magdeburg Horseman (ca 1240). In the background one can see the Church of St. John, now in ruins (1894).

Erfurt
The medieval Cathedral (left) and the Church of St. Severin, with the broad stairway leading up from the Cathedral square. The Petersberg and the hill on which the Cathedral stands are the dominant features of Erfurt's skyline (ca 1905).

Halberstadt
The medieval cathedral town of Halberstadt in the northern foothills of the Harz Mountains was founded in 827. Eighty per cent of the town was destroyed by bombing in 1945. The photograph, taken in 1898, shows the Fish Market and the Church of St. Martin.

Gotha
Built in 1892, this pavilion by the Schlossberg was designed as a piece of ornamental architecture to enhance the Leina canal (1911).

Chemnitz
A view of St. John's Square. The two raised platforms are for policemen directing the traffic. This architectural ensemble was almost completely destroyed by wartime bombing raids (1920/30).

tains, rocks or fast-flowing rivers; it is like a huge oasis in the ocean of sand which surrounds it on all sides, stretching all the way to Holland, Oldenburg and Cleves. Although it is extremely peaceful, it is very far from being a deserted wasteland: there can be few landscapes which have such an abundance of greenery, of flowers and birds; the traveller coming from less humid regions is almost deafened by the chattering of the countless songbirds who find their sustenance in the soft clay soil. The once-wild steppes have shrunk into moderately-sized meadows, each covered with a colourful carpet of wild flowers; with every step one takes, swarms of blue, yellow and milk-white butterflies flutter up into the air. In almost every one of these meadows there is a pond, garlanded with irises on which thousands of tiny dragonflies hang like brightly-coloured sticks, while the larger examples of the species fly out into the middle of the pond and settle, like golden decorative pins in little enamel bowls, on the leaves of the yellow water-lilies, where they lie in wait for the water-insects on which they feed. The meadows are bordered, in many cases, by small stretches of woodland. The trees are all of the deciduous variety; they include an impeccably beautiful stock of oak trees which supply wood for the masts of the Durch navy. Every tree contains a nest, on every branch there is a merrily chirping bird, and everywhere there is a freshness, a scent of greenery, which in other places one only finds immediately after a spring shower. In the shade of the trees, the elongated houses, whose roofs extend almost down to the ground, appear to be taking their midday rest, keeping a half-open eye on the cows, whose light colour, with markings like those of fallow deer, stands out clearly against the green of the woods and the paleness of the horizon. The cows move across the meadow in groups whose composition constantly changes: these moorland pastures are common land, and sixty animals or more graze on each section. The land which is not woodland or moorland is private property; it is divided into strips known as *Kämpe* which are used for pasturage or growing crops and which, depending on the size of the holding or the use to which it is put, are surrounded by high walls of earth topped with trees. This saves the owner the trouble of watching over his cattle to ensure that they do not stray. The soil of the *Kämpe* is particularly fertile; one generally finds these strips of land set in long rows, connected by narrow paths and little gates, and one enters them with an agreeable feeling of curiosity, as if one were walking through the rooms of a house with no roof. The meadows are an especially gay sight: they contain a richly variegated wealth of flowers and herbs, in the midst of which the massive Friesian cows, the élite breed of cattle, lie sated, chewing the cud and snorting at passers-by with the lazy arrogance which is the especial prerogative of these four-legged incarnations of lethargy. Here, as everywhere else, there are many ditches and ponds; as with all stagnant waters, their odour would be offensive were it not for the covering of white flowers, interspersed with forget-me-nots, which grow in profusion, and the aromatic scent of the wild mint, which largely counteract the smell. The banks of the sluggishly-flowing rivers are also adorned in this way, which allays the discomfort to which such rivers invariably give rise. In sum, this area offers an animated solitude, an opportunity of experiencing happiness in private communion with nature, which we have encountered nowhere else.

Annette von Droste-Hülshoff

Münster

Of all the towns in Westphalia, Münster is the most elegant; indeed, it has no equal in the whole of Germany. It has shed its carapace of walls and towers, and only two remnants of the medieval fortifications are left: the Buddenturm, a spectre from the distant past, surrounded by new streets, and the Zwinger, a splendid one-eyed rotunda whose form is enlivened by a coat of arms, a few windows and a staircase; its slate roof gives it an almost homelike appearance. However, the domestic garb which the city now wears is still rather like a suit of armour; its cut is severe, and the jewels with which it is adorned do not immediately catch the eye. In general, the houses are simple, but even the dwellings of the poor are not shabby or vulgar, and those of the rich are far from ostentatious. Where the aim is to express the spirit of the town as a whole, one finds displays of splendour, but they are tempered by the elegance of line which characterizes the buildings. Although the pediment of the town hall has a fiery grandeur, it also has a somewhat aloof, reticent quality; the red brick, which is much used in the town, is a deep burgundy colour, glowing like a fire that has been damped down by pride. Where there is exuberance, the effect is not of a loss of self-control, but of an abundance of beauty which is bound up with the obligations of wealth and aristocratic status. Münster is a town in whose coat of arms one would like to write the words which are to be found above the fireplace in the guildhall: *Ehr is dwang nog* (Honour is coercion enough).

The free man, who in bygone days was equated with the nobleman, will brook no coercion by others, but he imposes a stern discipline on himself.

Ricarda Huch

Dortmund

In my city, a tree in blossom is more than just a tree; it is a miracle which makes everyday life worth living.

The tree, the blossom, the fruit.

The history of my city stretches back over 1,000 years, but the city is new, as new as any place can be which was destroyed day by day over the six years of the last war, leaving people who crawled out of caves. It has no tradition; it is sober-sided, hard-working, dusty but clean - and devoid of charm.

My city is a big village, a conglomeration of villages, and these are the parts of it which I love. I hate the stench which always hangs over the city, but I love the people in the countless villages; I hate the city centre, which is flashy and upstart and uniform, but I love the bars in the village-like urban communities.

The whole of Dortmund is one vast bar: the next bar is never more than a hundred metres away, and there the men stand drinking their beer, chatting away for hours on end. If a stranger takes it into his head to ask them why on earth they don't sit down, the answer is invariably: because we haven't got the time.

My city sometimes stinks, and by "sometimes" I mean often. There are always smoke and fumes - pink, white and poison-yellow – coming from somewhere. There is always dust – brown, black and red. There is always noise: somewhere or other the beer is bound to be flowing, and people are singing and kicking up a racket: before and after the football match, in the bars, in the Westfalenhalle stadium. Even without the Westfalenhalle, Dortmund is a giant beer parlour.

The city is endless, stretching on for miles and miles to the north and south, and even further to the east and west. One village, or suburb, follows another; the roads are like nylon strings on which the villages are threaded to make up what is commonly called a city.

Cows graze by the coal tips, the mountains of the modern age; a farmer ploughs his field next to a giant colliery; in the city centre there are traffic jams throughout the day, not only in the rush hour; a few hundred metres farther on, a shepherd drives his flock across a main road: the cars and trams stop, and suddenly everyone has time on their hands: the restless people regain their sight.

The local football team has lost a match, and a television set flies out of a third-floor window in Borsigplatz; the iron is being run off at the Hoesch steelworks; coal is being cut from a seam 800 metres below the hospital for accident cases; in the northern part of the city, invalid miners with silicosis are exercising their lungs, which have their own place in local history. A bosses' meeting is taking place on the Hohensyburg; ladies of advanced years are convening for coffee. Along the urban motorway live Germany's young millionaires, on whose decision hangs the fate of ten thousand unemployed workers, all hoping to find a job. In the south, the university – at once a symbol of progress and a nightmare – towers above the fields.

My city has many faces. Its appearance does not only change with the seasons: it wears different faces at different times of the day. In the early morning it is a city of workers; later on it becomes a city of businessmen; at midday it is a city of youth; in the evening it is a city of haste and bustle; at night it is a city of drinkers.

On Sundays, parents take their children to the Westfalenpark, where other people exercise their dogs. In the suburb of Eving, a girl washes the dust off the shrubs in her garden with soap and water. She is happy because, for an hour at least, green will once more become green and red will be red. Even on warm days, the sun does not really shine here: between the sun and the city there is always a veil, rising up from countless chimneys.

The women are resourceful: instead of hanging the washing outside, they dry it in the cellar or the attic. And in the allotments – of which there are also vast numbers – the hosepipes wash off the residue of industry: a victory which lasts only a few hours.

In our city there is also culture. The community is divided into two classes of people: those who thirst after culture and those who can afford it.

My city is governed by the SPD, but that means nothing at all. To a certain extent, the people of Dortmund are proud of their city, especially of the breweries, which spread the city's fame all over the world. This boosts people's self-confidence when they travel abroad.

My city is a clean and tidy place. The men wear ties and white shirts every day of the week, and people are probably better-dressed than anywhere else: the dust from the pits and factories is a positive challenge to keep oneself spruce and neat. The women here clean their windows at least twice a week....

People have learned to live with the dust, the polluted air and the sun which never wins the constant battle with the fumes.

On Sundays, a pall of boredom hangs over the city centre. The people have driven out into the country, to the Sauerland or the Münsterland. For the sake of a few hours spent breathing clean air, they are prepared to put up with the endless traffic jams.

The people of my city are by no means spendthrift, but they are hospitable and generous: if a stranger joins in their conversation in a bar, they will often buy him a beer. They are prepared to live and let live; they are tolerant as long as nobody contradicts them.

The people of Dortmund heave a sigh of relief when they come back from their holidays and re-enter the atmosphere of the city. The holiday was restful and relaxing: they have been to the seaside or the mountains and acquired a suntan, so they at least have something to show for the whole exercise - but all they want do now is to get the car unloaded as quickly as possible. The wife unpacks the cases, thinking – perhaps a trifle wistfully – of the holiday resort they have just left, and tidies up the house (in her absence, one of the neighbours will have been looking after the plants, and possibly the dog as well). Meanwhile her husband nips over the road to the bar, just to see what's going on, to drink a beer, play a quick game of cards or dice and stand everybody a round of Schnaps. This is the standard procedure when you have been away and come back: it is a ritual which also satisfies a heartfelt need. Nowhere in the world does Dortmund beer taste better than in Dortmund itself.

Max von der Grün

Bonn

The seat of government is the building over which the big black, red and gold flag flies. The Federal Parliament is a huge factory, in which bills of minor and major importance are busily and heatedly debated; they are chopped about, turned this way and that, shaped and re-shaped, cut up and put back together, until they finally leave the apparatus and enter the statute book as instruments of power.

The Federal Parliament stands like a white giant by the Rhine; it is surrounded by gardens and by other, cube-shaped buildings. The promenade by the Rhine is lined with innocent poplars and ancient beech trees which date back beyond the time of Ernst Moritz Arndt and Heinrich Heine; their leaves rustle in the summer breeze. From the windows of the Parliament building one can watch the barges which haul up and down the Rhine, between Holland and Switzerland. The economy is in full swing: industry and trade are booming. Bonn supplies the politics to match. But down on the promenade, one may see an old professor taking a stroll, clasping his umbrella behind his back and pondering on some detail of Indo-Germanic etymology. Students cycle up the river to their boathouse. Busloads of tourists marvel at the Parliament building, their heads turning to the left or to the right, following the guide's explanations. Nuns drift past, bulky in their black habits. Or there may be a small group of deputies, walking up and down and talking in angry voices.

On the other side of the Parliament building there are the four offices reserved for the press. In scores of tiny rooms, the accredited jounalists sit sweating at their telephones, filing their reports to newspapers, news agencies and radio stations.

Günther Weisenborn

Cologne Cathedral

Between 1850 and 1920, Cologne saw an era of prosperity and growth under the aegis of several well-known mayors, including Hermann and Wilhelm Becker, Max Wallraf and Konrad Adenauer, who was elected in 1917. The grandest event of this whole period was the festival held to celebrate the completion of the Cathedral in 1880...

The first meeting of the Cathedral Building Association took place on 14 February 1842 in the Gürzenich, an assembly hall and ballroom dating back to 1447. In December, the Berlin Society for Cologne Cathedral presented Luther's wedding ring to the Association, a gesture which clearly indicated the popularity, even among Protestants, of the movement to rebuild the Cathedral. It was supported by the lower and higher orders alike. Ludwig I, the King of Bavaria, donated a set of stained-glass windows, and the Rhineland Railway company similarly immortalized itself in the south transept. The women's clubs of Cologne contributed carpets made according to a design by J.J. Ramboux. Aid for the Cathedral came from a wide variety of different sources. The enthusiasm persisted, although in the course of time it was somewhat dampened by political frictions, and the records also speak of attempts to make private profit out of the undertaking, in which vanity and other petty human weaknesses played their customary part.

On 4 September 1842, Friedrich Wilhelm IV of Prussia laid the foundation-stone for the completion of the building. This event was not the result of a sudden, ad hoc decision. Thirty years previously, the scholar and art-collector Sulpiz Boisserée had begun to devote his energies to the Cathedral. Boisserée was a cosmopolitan at heart: as a young man with an exceptionally lively intellect, he fled the narrowness of his native city, and throughout his life he remained a restless wanderer. Görres and others joined him in the movement to complete the Cathedral.

Boisserée pressured and lobbied and compiled a portfolio of large-format sketches based on the torso of the Cathedral which he published in 1821. Above all, he recruited Goethe as a supporter of the bold undertaking. Romantic nostalgia for the Middle Ages, assisted by the reawakening of nationalism and the idea of Empire, activated the Zeitgeist.

Fearing a revival of the German myth, the aged Metternich felt decidedly uneasy when Friedrich Wilhelm IV proclaimed at the foundation ceremony: "May this great work speak to future generations as a testimony of a Germany made great and powerful by the unity of its princes and peoples, enforcing world peace by unbloody means." The Prussian King was fond of such gaudy, glittering platitudes, which found a ready audience of professional applauders.

The inhabitants of the medieval city saw the Cathedral as a heavenly Jerusalem. The nineteenth century made it into a national monument, a symbol of German unity and power.

The names, facts and dates from the forty years between the initiation of the project and its completion are quickly enumerated. The most important name is that of the first architect, Ernst Zwirner, who came from Silesia. In 1852 the King inserted the keystone above the front arch at the main door on the west side. The south

Festivities

Altes Land
Young people in traditional costume near Steinkirchen, keeping old customs alive as a matter of course.

On the island of Amrum
Celebrating the summer solstice on this North Frisian island that was a Danish enclave until the middle of the 19th century.

Wismar
These actors in period dress, pausing between takes for a film of a novel by Thomas Mann, offer a nostalgic glimpse into the history of Wismar, a former Hanseatic town on the Baltic coast.

Munich
Beer tent at the Oktoberfest. The beer as well as all the other attractions pull in the crowds from all over the world at the end of September.

Nuremberg
View of the Christmas Market in Nuremberg. Originally famous for its special spiced biscuits, it has now become a tourist attraction in its own right.

Cologne
During Carnival-time the fools are on the loose, with the whole of the city centre as their stage.

Wasungen
Carnival is not only celebrated in the Rhineland: this picture shows a group of Carnival jesters in Wasungen, a small town on the edge of the Forest of Thuringia.

door was completed in 1855. There were various squabbles concerning the ridge turret: as Boisserée's sketches show, this had been the subject of controversy right from the outset. Finally, in 1860, the crossing was given "a crown of iron with a lead mantle", which in the view of later critics was "still too big and heavy". The partition wall between the chancel and the nave, which the poet Karl Simrock called "evil", was removed in 1863, making it possible to see the whole interior of the Cathedral at a single glance. Zwirner did not live to see this "miracle": he died in 1861. The city of Cologne still honours his memory: he is buried in Melaten cemetery, where his grave is decorated with a medallion carved by Christian Mohr and covered with a huge stone slab which has an almost monumental quality.

Art historians subsequently levelled a good deal of criticism at the architects, sculptors and painters who worked on the Cathedral. Their efforts were contemptuously dismissed as "amateur Gothic", even by those scholars who took Neo-Gothic architecture at all seriously. However, these criticisms are now a thing of the past. These days, nobody disputes that the restorers, Johann Ramboux, Christian Mohr, Peter Fuchs and Eduard von Steinle, were fine craftsmen with a highly individual artistic sense. The Neo-Gothic style was more than mere "industrial" pastiche: it had its own distinctive signature and creative flair.

Zwirner was succeeded by Richard Voigtel, a native of Magdeburg. In 1868, the crane which had been used in the building work was removed; it had stood by the Cathedral for so long that it had become a familiar sight, a kind of landmark to the inhabitants of the city and a standard motif in local artists' paintings and etchings of the Rhine promenade.

In extending the west façade, Zwirner was probably helped by the original sketches from the fourteenth century, one of which had been found in 1814 by an architect named Möller in the attic of an inn in Darmstadt. This auspicious event was followed by a second stroke of luck: parts of a further drawing, which augmented the one from Darmstadt, came to light in the Bibliothèque Nationale in Paris.

The idea of the Cathedral as a national monument was given a further boost in 1875 by the addition of the "Emperor's Bell", cast from the bronze of cannons captured in the Franco-Prussian War of 1870-71. It was the biggest church bell in the world. This patriotic showpiece, with its decidedly martial overtones, was melted down in 1918, when Germany was preparing for what the generals claimed would be the final and decisive offensive on the Western front. "Peace through victory" was the mendacious slogan of the day: nothing but hocus-pocus, for the war was already lost.

Fired by the enthusiasm surrounding the festivities to celebrate the completion of the Cathedral, Wilhem Schneider-Clauss wrote his famous dialect song "Alaaf Kölle". Cologne had come a long way, and the grand historical procession on 16 October 1880 was a fitting demonstration of the city's pride in its achievements.

The Second Empire stood at the zenith of its power. One can only be thankful that the bizarre proposal to build a "Kaiserstrasse" leading directly to the Cathedral was never implemented. It is bad enough that the railway station and the Rhine bridge were sited so close to the chancel: a crassly mistaken piece of town planning of which nobody could really approve. But it was too late to rectify the situation. Such errors are part of a general process of depersonalization which began in the early years of the twentieth century and which the historian Jacob Burckhardt anticipated with deep foreboding.

Max Leo Schwering

Carnival in Cologne

The people here are happy and fun-loving: I like them greatly and have got to know many of them very quickly. But they are nothing like the people of earlier times! What amuses me best is, of course, the city itself: latterly I have been studying the chronicles of Cologne and reading a great deal about the buildings and works of art. But I haven't turned Catholic, whatever Aug. v. Cölln may say. I must admit that I found Carl's architectural plans strange. But he is old enough to be his own counsellor. I should be sorry if he got into trouble: let us hope that the maiden Elisabeth, the district president's daughter, will keep him in check, then perhaps things will turn out right after all. I was truly pleased about your parliament. Even the smallest state can assert its rights, and there is no harm in giving one of the thirty-six monarchs a good hiding now and again - otherwise the good ones will get too big for their breeches!

Here, the carnival tomfoolery is in full swing. Every Sunday there is a meeting of one of the "committees", where 600 people, young and old, rich and poor, with silly hats on their swaying heads, assemble – not to discuss the welfare of the country but to debate how they are going to amuse themselves for the next few hours. There is no finer sight than this happy mass of people. The tables and benches are superfluous: everybody hangs his bottle round his neck and keeps his glass in his hand in order to cheer or hiss at the speakers who bawl away in Cologne dialect on the platform. And then the whole crowd sings "O Jerum! O Jerum!", a song without words. Thirty brass instruments strike up with a mighty blare. The people go into a frenzy and lose their wits entirely; they all embrace each other, greybeards and young men alike; in a word, it is mad, mad, mad!

But now the Cathedral bell tolls. Everybody disperses – and since the night is still young, the innkeepers earn yet more money, for most of the revellers continue wandering from one tavern to another, until they return, with drooping heads, to their usual labours on Monday morning. O Jerum! O Jerum!

Georg Weerth

Dresden, the German Florence

The road from Meissen to Dresden is planted with Egyptian thorn and pear-trees; the fields are covered with cabbages and potatoes: it is a complete kitchen-garden! Charming vineyards and leafy woods lie on both sides. With its palace and its Gothic cathedral, Meissen itself, which stands on a hill, forms the finest point in the whole picture. A stone bridge rises over the Elbe, below the town, where people drive and walk, without thinking about, or much less priding themselves on, the life they thereby give to the whole.

The farther we recede from here, the higher the mountains become; and we soon see, as though through a bluish veil, the German Florence. Dresden lies before us, with its high towers and domes.

When I reached the Augustus Bridge, which I knew so well from engravings, it appeared to me as if I had, in a dream, been here once before. The Elbe poured out its yellow waves under the proud arches; there was life and bustle on the river, but still more on the bridge; carriages and horsemen went rapidly over it, and on both sides there was a great variety of foot-passengers. Approximately in the middle of the river, on one of the piers which form the single arches, stood a metal crucifix...

With Dahl, our Danish ambassador, and the two Norwegians, I went to the picture-gallery. In some of the rooms the paintings lay on the floor, but in most of them they were already arranged and hung. What a mass of works of art!

What should I say first about the great productions that made the deepest impression on me? But surely there can be no question: Raphael's Madonna!

I hurried through the rooms in search of this painting, and when I stood before it, it did not surprise me at all. It appeared to be a friendly female face, but not more beautiful than many I had seen. Is this the world's far-famed picture I wondered, and wished to be surprised on seeing it, but it remained the same. It even appeared to me that several paintings of the Madonna, several female faces here in the gallery, were far prettier. I returned to it again, and then the veil fell from my eyes: the others now appeared to me as painted human faces, for I had seen divinity itself. I again stood before her, and it was only then that I sensed the endless truth and glory in this picture. There is nothing in it that takes one aback, nothing that dazzles one, but the more attentively one regards her and the infant Jesus, the more divine do they become. No woman has such a super-human, childlike face, and yet it is pure nature. It appeared to me as if every pious, innocent girl's face had some resemblance to it, but that this was the ideal after which all the others strove. Not love, but adoration, called forth that look. It now became intelligible to me how a rationally-minded Catholic can kneel before an image. It is not the colours on the canvas that he worships, it is the spirit, the divine spirit which reveals itself here in a corporeal form to the bodily eye, while the powerful tones of the organ peal above him and chase away the discords of the soul, so that a harmony arises between the earthly and the eternal.

Time has paled the colours of this painting, but all of the figures seem to live: the great halo of angels' heads behind develop themselves more and more, and in the look of the infant Jesus we see the whole grand expression comprised. Such a look, such a wise eye, is not to be found in any child; and yet here it is natural childishness which impresses us so powerfully. And then the angel children below; they stand as a beautiful type of earthly innocence; the younger one looks forward with the calmness of childhood, while the elder one raises his eyes to the heavenly figures above him. This picture alone would make the gallery famous, just as it has sufficed to make its master immortal.

Hans Christian Andersen

The Destruction of Dresden

During the destruction of Dresden on the evening of 13 February 1945, I was sitting in an air-raid shelter in Berlin, looking at a tattered blueprint of a map of Germany and listening to the microphone heroes of Berlin Command, who spoke of swarms of enemy bombers and reeled off a list of map coordinates which told me that my home city was in the process of being obliterated. Meanwhile, my parents were sitting in a cellar in that very city...

This September, I went back home for the first time since Christmas 1944...

The city which used to be known as Dresden no longer exists. Walking through it is like walking in a dream through Sodom and Gomorrah. Now and then, a tram passes through the dream, clattering and jangling. In this desert of rubble there is no place for human beings: crossing it, one has the feeling of going from one shore to another, with only death in between. Between Nürnberger Platz, far beyond the main station, and Albertplatz in the newer part of the city, not a single house remains standing. This is a trek of some forty minutes. It takes almost twice as long to cross the desert which extends in the other direction, parallel to the Elbe. Fifteen square kilometres of the city have been mown down and blown away. If you walk along the narrow trail which was once renowned all over the world as Prager Strasse, you find yourself starting at the sound of your own footsteps. For miles round, you see nothing but hills and valleys of rubble and stone: a dusty landscape of broken masonry. Odd corners of houses and slender chimneys stick out of the wreckage like isolated trees in a wasteland. The narrow lanes, where rows of houses have collapsed into one another as if they had fallen into each other's arms at the moment of death, have been blocked off with barricades of rubble. Ruined churches lie beached, like the wrecks of huge ships blown ashore by a cyclone. The gutted towers of the Kreuzkirche, the Hofkirche, the Town Hall and the Palace look like chopped-down masts. The golden statue of Hercules above the gaunt skeleton of the Town Hall's domed roof makes one think of a figurehead: in a mysterious manner, which is the stuff of legends, it has withstood the fiery typhoon. The stone shrouds and spars of the stranded giants have melted like lead in the heat of the whirlwind. In a single night, a geological metamorphosis has been wrought which would otherwise be the work of aeons.

At the edges of the vast desert, one enters those parts of the city where there is still life and space to breathe among the ruins. Here, the scene is much like that in other bombed-out cities. However, every single one of the villas in the area around the Grosser Garten has been gutted. Even the Palais and the little Cavalier's House in the middle of the park have been razed. As a student, I sometimes dreamed of achieving fame and honour. In my dream, the mayor appeared before me and offered me the opportunity of living for the rest of my life in one of these enchanting little one-storey Baroque houses, in recognition of my services as a valiant son of the city. From the window, I would have had a view of the the lake and the incomparable flower-beds; I would have watched the swans and the squirrels. The blue tits would have come flying into my room to share my breakfast. Ah, the dreams of youth! The pond has been drained and is overgrown with weeds. The swans have flown away, just as the dream has evaporated. The flames have even charred the solitary bench in the quietest corner of the park, where couples once sat and looked up at the moon floating above the treetops; around it, the grass grows wild.

I spent a whole day walking the length and breadth of the city, pursuing my memories of the past. My school? Gutted...The seminary where I spent all those dull years as a boarder? An empty façade...The Dreikönigskirche, where I was baptised and confirmed? Where in the autumn, the starlings, exhausted by their practice flights, fell out of the trees in screeching black clouds? The tower stands in a void, looking like a giant pencil...The library in the Japanese Palace, where I slaved over my doctoral thesis? Ruined...The Frauenkirche, the wonderful old church where I sometimes joined the choir to sing motets? A few wretched remnants of masonry...The Opera? The Europäischer Hof? The Alberttheater? The Café Kreutzkamm with its Christmas cakes which smelled so delicious? The Hotel Bellevue? The Zwinger? The museum of local history?And the other places whose memory held a special significance for me alone? Gone, all gone.

Friends had told me: "Don't go. You won't be able to bear it." I examined my reactions with care, checking the level of pain. It does not rise with the number of wounds; it very quickly reaches a critical limit, and one ceases to feel any pain which follows. It is as if one's heart had fallen into a deep swoon.

Erich Kästner

Frankfurt

Frankfurt had two faces: it was both the city of money and the historic city where the Holy Roman Emperors were crowned. In Goethe's day, and even as late as 1848, when Frankfurt became the capital city of an Empire which existed only in the realm of ideas, the general atmosphere of the place was contented and relaxed; although the attitude of the city's rulers was at times stiff and unyielding, this was offset by the independent spirit of the burghers, who were quietly aware of their own strength. Rulers and citizens alike clung to the proud traditions of the past: they were united in their loyalty to the old Empire and their aversion to Prussian rule, which had been thrust upon them against their will. When in 1867 the tower of the Cathedral where the Emperors had formerly been crowned caught fire and collapsed, this loss of a familiar landmark seemed to symbolize the eclipse of former glories and the passing of a happy way of life.

Initially, the new era brought pompous monuments and buildings overloaded with vulgar ornamentation; the restrained elegance of the Baroque palaces on the Zeil was obliged to make way for pretentious, ugly business premises. However, notwithstanding all the beauty which disappeared and the tastelessness which replaced it, many parts of Frankfurt have retained their character of serene majesty. Between the Cathedral and the Romerberg, there are a number of quaint little shops with awnings and bow windows, intimate courtyards, and tiny squares with fountains, all of which have recently been painted in a manner which discreetly reveals their structure and gives them a quite captivating charm. The very names of the streets - names such as Five-Finger Corner, Rapunzel Alley, Gold Hat Lane, Behind the Lambkin, Golden Lion Square - transport the wanderer into a world of children's fairytales. In the vicinity of the Eschenheim Tower, the main land-

**Germany in
Old photographs,
1850-1920:
From Cologne
to Munich**

Cologne
An idyllic view of the Haymarket in Cologne, with the tower of St. Martin's Church to be glimpsed in the background (ca 1880).

Cologne
Grand view of the Rhine around 1855 looking towards Cologne Cathedral, at that time still not completed. On the far left is the tower of the Town Hall, on the far right the former Jesuit Church of the Assumption. The centre of the picture is taken up by the old fish and meat market.

Düsseldorf
Fountains with sculptures on the Stadtgraben, around 1910.

Wiesbaden
View from the Neroberg of this famous spa. With its twenty-seven mineral springs, it has attracted people to take the waters since Roman times (1890).

Mainz
Panoramic view of Mainz as seen from the Rhine (ca 1919).

Stuttgart
Fine half-timbered buildings line Stuttgart's Market Square (ca 1900).

Augsburg
View of Augsburg from the south (before 1914). The town owed its influential position as an industrial and financial centre to the extensive and far-sighted economic policy of the Fugger family.

Munich
View of Maximilianstrasse. This monumental avenue leading from the National Theatre to the embankment of the Isar was built in the 1850s during the reign of Maximilian II. The English-style neo-Gothic buildings today house the most exclusive shops in Munich (1910).

Munich
A birds-eye view of the old town in about 1885 from the tower of St. Peter's Church taking in Marienplatz, the narrow row of houses forming Kaufingerstrasse and the Cathedral.

mark of Frankfurt, one still finds rows of noble façades; Goethe's house and its surroundings take us back to the days when the wealthy burghers held sway, whose inherited talents and industry led them to place themselves on a par with princes. One hopes that the countenance of the historic city will be preserved - may its grace and charm continue for ever to radiate through the flamboyance of the new city.

Ricarda Huch

Nuremberg

We are in the city of Nuremberg. "City" is the operative word, for Nuremberg has an especially striking urban quality. It is also a city with a hidden, very definite order, stemming from its character and its history: rather than walking through it at random, one is unconsciously drawn along by a particular force, corresponding to the spirit of a city which willingly opens itself up to the stranger. This is one of Nuremberg's truly remarkable beauties: its way of insinuating itself into one's nervous system, into the presentiments which direct one's path, and forcing one to take this or that route. If I am at the Lorenzkirche, I have no option but to walk over to the Fleischbrücke, with its ox carved in stone; in the middle of the bridge, I have to stand and look at the bright colours of the washing hanging out to dry, and at the opaque, yellowish-olive waters of the River Pegnitz, which flows sluggishly past. Then I simply have to visit the market, with its wonderful smell of fresh vegetables; my attention is divided between the Frauenkirche, over to the right of the broad square, and the splendid chancel of the Sebaldskirche up on the left. Following this, before doing anything else, I have to climb up to the Castle. From here, I refresh my memory, with renewed pleasure, of the old steeply-sloping roofs, whose colour varies between a fiery red and a blackish hue, and which look like an accumulation of waves that have coagulated and set fast in a kind of dream. One of the towers of the Sebaldskirche is vitriol-green, just as I remember it. The roofs are similar to those in Strasbourg when seen from one of the towers of the Minster: the view is the same, exciting yet tranquil. At times, the tiles look like the scales of a fish: this is especially the case today, for they are still wet from the rain which fell earlier on. The historic centre of the city is surrounded by a ring of industry, with factories and smoking chimneys. When I turn round, I see the familiar black shape of the Castle tower, rearing up towards a sky which has begun to take on the delicate clearness of spring. All the while, the city itself guides my steps; this city which, for all its bourgeois uniformity, has such an eminently personal quality. There are few variations in the route, and quite automatically, I am prevented from missing a single one of the attractions which are unique to the city, no matter whether I see it in the winter, when at night, the white snow lends everything a wholly unreal beauty, or on a March day such as this, when at noon, the first yellow and green buds are painted on the ancient walls whose blackness is shot through with blood red. Nothing is left out: neither the little footbridge known as the Executioner's Bridge, nor the toy-like miniature town of the fleamarket, nor the hop warehouse with its stimulating fragrance, nor the Sankt-Ägidius-Kirche with the broad square on which it stands. I have never used a map in Nuremberg: everything has always presented itself automatically, and my feet have invariably followed the magnetic pull of the force which is such an attractive, and at the same time eerie, feature of the city.

Wilhelm Hausenstein

The Big Small Town: Tübingen

Tübingen: the small university town wrapped in provincial obscurity - a miniature rustic Heidelberg, with no court, no patrician élite, no class of self-assertive burghers, no society of distinguished citizens whose mental horizons extend beyond the bounds of the region. This is one side of Tübingen, but the town has another, quite different face: that of the global *polis*, the fountainhead of ideas which changed the world. Tübingen: the centre of intellectual life, whose significance becomes plain when one tries to imagine what would have happened if the town and its university had never existed. Kepler, as a young student, would never have learned the art of combining boldness with exactness in scientific speculation. Melanchthon, Brenz, Camerarius, Sichard and Fuchs, the five eminent theologians whose reforming zeal also extended to a wide variety of other fields, would not have assembled in the autumn of 1536 to hold their grand *colloquium spirituale*. Hölderlin, Hegel and Schelling would never have met in the Tübingen seminary; indeed, the seminary itself, a major centre of Protestantism, a counterweight to Salzburg and Sanssouci, would never have come into being. Ferdinand-Christian Baur would have been unable to teach the critical form of Biblical exegesis which liberated Christianity from the shackles of orthodoxy, in the very region which at that time was the centre of orthodox belief. Friedrich Theodor Vischer would never have lectured to audiences numbering several hundred, nor would Friedrich List have addressed the mere handful of students who attended his classes. There would have been no Cotta, the son of an old-established family of booksellers, to receive the manuscripts sent to him from Weimar; hence the German classical authors would have been without a publisher. Without the medical services of Dr Autenrieth, Hölderlin would have vanished into oblivion somewhere between Hesse and Swabia. Johann Valentin Andreä would have been unable to write his *Christianopolis*, and Wilhelm Hauff's

Devil would never have had the opportunity of studying theology in Tübingen - which would truly be a crying shame. Ernst Bloch, following in the footsteps of both Andreä and Hegel, would not have been able to return to the town where, once upon a time, three rebellious students at the seminary are said to have erected a maypole in the market square. And one of the most moving letters in the German language, the carpenter Zimmer's description of the mad Hölderlin, which must rank on a par with Waiblinger's portrait of the poet, would have remained unwritten.

Walter Jens

Heidelberg

Heidelberg lies at the mouth of a narrow gorge – a gorge the shape of a shepherd's crook; if one looks up it he perceives that it is about straight, for a mile and a half, then makes a sharp curve to the right and disappears. This gorge, – along whose bottom pours the swift Neckar, – is confined between (or cloven through) a couple of long, steep ridges, a thousand feet high and densely wooded clear to their summits, with the exception of one section which has been shaved and put under cultivation. These ridges are chopped off at the mouth of the gorge and form two bold and conspicuous headlands, with Heidelberg nestling between them; from their bases spreads away the vast dim expanse of the Rhine valley, and into this expanse the Neckar goes wandering in shining curves and is presently lost to view.

Now if one turns and looks up the gorge once more, he will see the Schloss Hotel on the right, perched on a precipice overlooking the Neckar, – a precipice which is so sumptuously cushioned and draped with foliage that no glimpse of the rock appears. The building seems very airily situated. It has the appearance of being on a shelf half way up the wooded mountain side; and as it is remote and isolated, and very white, it makes a strong mark against the lofty leafy rampart at its back.

This hotel had a feature which was a decided novelty, and one which might be adopted with advantage by any house which is perched in a commanding situation. This feature may be described as a series of glass-enclosed parlors *clinging to the outside of the house,* one against each and every bedchamber and drawing-room. They are like long, narrow, high-ceiled birdcages hung against the building. My room was a corner room, and had two of these things, a north one and a west one.

From the north cage one looks up the Neckar gorge; from the west one he looks down it. This last affords the most extensive view, and it is one of the loveliest that can be imagined, too. Out of a billowy upheaval of vivid green foliage, a rifle-shot removed, rises the huge ruin of Heidelberg Castle, with empty window arches, ivy-mailed battlements, moldering towers – the Lear of inanimate nature, – deserted, discrowned, beaten by the storms, but royal still, and beautiful. It is a fine sight to see the evening sunlight suddenly strike the leafy declivity at the Castle's base and dash up it and drench it as with a luminous spray, while the adjacent groves are in deep shadow.

Behind the Castle swells a great dome-shaped hill, forest-clad, and beyond that a nobler and loftier one. The Castle looks down upon the compact brown-roofed town; and from the town two picturesque old bridges span the river. Now the view broadens; through the gateway of the sentinel headlands you gaze out over the wide Rhine plain, which stretches away, softly and richly tinted, grows gradually and dreamily indistinct, and finally melts imperceptibly into the remote horizon.

Mark Twain

Munich was radiant

Munich was radiant. Above the gay squares and white columned temples, the classicistic monuments and the baroque churches, the leaping fountains, the palaces and parks of the Residence there stretched a sky of luminous blue silk. Well-arranged leafy vistas laced with sun and shade lay basking in the sunshine of a beautiful day in early June.

There was a twittering of birds and a blithe holiday spirit in all the little streets. And in the squares and past the rows of villas there swelled, rolled, and hummed the leisurely, entertaining traffic of that easy-going, charming town. Travellers of all nationalities drove about in the slow little droshkies, looking right and left in aimless curiosity at the house-fronts; they mounted and descended museum stairs...

Indolent, unhurried sauntering was the mode in all the long streets of the northern quarter. There life is lived for pleasanter ends than the driving greed of gain. Young artists with little round hats on the backs of their heads, flowing cravats and nocanes – carefree bachelors who paid for their lodgings with colour-sketches – were strolling up and down to let the clear blue morning play upon their mood, also to look at the little girls, the pretty, rather plump type, with the brunette bandeaux, the too large feet, and the unobjectionable morals. Every fifth house had studio windows blinking in the sun. Sometimes a fine piece of architecture stood out from a middle-class row, the work of some imaginative young architect; a wide front with shallow bays and decorations in a bizarre style very expressive and full of invention. Or the door to some monotonous facade would be framed in a bold improvisation of flowing lines and sunny colours, with bacchantes, naiads, and rosy-skinned nudes.

It was always a joy to linger before the windows of the cabinet-makers and the shops for modern articles *de luxe*. What a sense for luxurious nothings and amusing, significant line was displayed in the shape of everything! Little shops that sold picture-frames, sculptures, and antiques there were in endless number; in their windows you might see those busts of Florentine women of the Renaissance, so full of noble poise and poignant charm. And the owners of the smallest and meanest of these shops spoke of Mino da Fiesole and Donatello as though he had received the rights of reproduction from them personally...

You might be lucky enough to meet in person one of the famous fair ones whom less fortunate folk know only through the medium of art; one of those rich and beautiful women whose Titian-blond colouring Nature's most sweet and cunning hand did *not* lay on, but whose diamond parures and beguiling charms had received immortality from the hand of some portrait-painter of genius and whose love-affairs were the talk of the town. These were the queens of the artist balls at carnival time. They were a little painted, a little made up, full of haughty caprices, worthy of adoration, avid of praise. You might see a carriage rolling up the Ludwigstrasse, with such a great painter and his mistress inside. People would be pointing out the sight, standing still to gaze after the pair. Some of them would curtsy. A little more and the very policemen would stand at attention.

Art flourished, art swayed the destinies of the town, art stretched above it her rose-bound sceptre and smiled. On every hand obsequious interest was displayed in her prosperity, on every hand she was served with industry and devotion. There was a down-right cult of line, decoration, form, significance, beauty. Munich was radiant.

Thomas Mann

Old Bavaria

Old Bavaria was not a rich land. It contained the ruins of four mountain systems. These had caused many disturbances in their time, now the surface was quiet at last, and subject to no more tremors. But the land's treasures, the coal and metals, had sunk so far down that they could not be utilised.

The country possessed height and spaciousness, had mountains, lakes and rivers. Its skies were brilliant, its air gave a glow to all colours. It was a part of the world that was good to look upon, as it sloped from the Alps to the Danube.

The inhabitants of the country from time immemorial had been peasants, hostile to the towns. They loved their fields. They were stubborn and strong, with keen perceptions, but weak judgments. Their needs were small; but what they had they held on to with tooth and nail. Slow and stubborn-minded, they were unwilling to labour for future benefits, and clung to their existing rude comforts and pleasures. They loved the past, were content with the present, and hated the future. They gave to their settlements good, homely names, they built houses on which the eye could dwell with pleasure, and embellished them with solid ornamentation. They loved arts and crafts of all kinds, and had a feeling for gay costumes, festivals, comic shows, church decorations, processions, for abundant meat and drink, for orgies of fighting. They loved, too, mountain-climbing and hunting.

The centre of this country, Munich, was a huge village with but little industry. It contained a thin, liberal stratum of feudal lords and leading citizens, a small number of the proletariat, and a large lower middle-class still very closely connected with the peasantry. The town was beautiful; its princes had embellished it with rich collections and fine architecture; it possessed palaces of grace and good dimensions, churches of an intimate and moving charm. It had many green places, great beer gardens with pleasant views of river and mountain. In fine shops were exposed for sale the charming patriarchal furniture of an earlier period, and entertaining knick-knacks of all sorts. The city was based economically on brewing, arts and crafts, banking, timber, and the corn and fruit trade. It produced good applied art, and the best beer in the world. Otherwise it offered little material for industrial development. The more active intellects always left the town; they were recruited from among late-born sons of peasants who, following the old tradition, had no claim to a patrimony. Since the fall of the dynasty the feudal aristocracy, too, had withdrawn more and more, the Arco-Valleys, the Ottingen-Wallersteins, the Castell-Castells, the Poschingers and Torrings. Few rich people remained. Only one man in ten thousand was taxed on a capital of one million marks or over. For the rest the city lived a noisy, careless life of good-natured sensuality. It was content with itself. Its watchwords were: Build, brew, be merry.

Three centuries before this the chronicler Johann Turmair, better known as Aventinus, had said of his countrymen that they were plain and honest, listened to their priests, stayed preferably at home, and travelled little. They were hard drinkers and had big families. Were more devoted to their crops and farm-stock than to fighting. They were surly, self-willed and obstinate. They looked down on the merchants, and did little trading. The average Bavarian did as he liked, drank beer day and night, shouted, sang, danced and played at cards. He liked long knives and other instruments of offence. He considered he had a right to prolonged and noisy wedding feasts, funerals and church festivals, and nobody grudged him these.

Lion Feuchtwanger

Up the Rhine

On the banks of the river Rhine
Rhine scenery near Coblenz, where the river broadens in the valley of the Middle Rhine.

Bonn
Street café in the market square. Bounded by Rhine and Gumme, the old town of Bonn exudes a carefully restored patrician charm.

Kaub am Rhein
Situated on the right bank of the Rhine, Kaub is dominated by Gutenfels Castle which as a European Youth Centre today attracts visitors from all over the world.

Düsseldorf
The meeting of old and new – a pastoral scene against a backdrop of the last word in modern bridge architecture.

Loreley near Sankt Goarshausen
The much-sung rock towers a precipitous 132 metres above the Rhine by Sankt Goarshausen. According to legend, shipping was at the mercy of the beautiful nymph; in fact the danger came from the reefs and the fast-flowing waters.

Pfalz near Kaub am Rhein
A former toll castle of the Palatine Electorate dating back to the first half of the 14th century situated on a rocky island in the middle of the river.

Bad Ems an der Lahn
Famous for its springs,
this spa lies between wooded
hills on the left and right
bank of the Lahn.

By the Middle Rhine
Perched on a wooded hill-top, just one of the many castles to be found along the Rhine.

square kilometres which made up the area called Salzgitter, the biggest deposit of iron ore in Germany had been discovered, at a time when the self-styled Third Reich needed iron for the war. It had blood enough.

In July 1937 the "Reichswerke A.G. für Erzbergbau und Eisenhütten Hermann Göring" were founded. Five years later, on March 31, 1942, the city of Salzgitter was founded by official decree. But to win the war, the Third Reich would have needed far more iron ore than the mines of Salzgitter could provide. And the ore was of poor quality, so-called "acid" ore.

Along with the rest of the assets from the bankruptcy of the Third Reich, the Federal government took over Salzgitter and the "Reichswerke", as they are still called (the "Hermann Göring" has been dropped). And optimists say that the day will come when they and the other shareholders who have subsequently bought a stake in the company will hit the jackpot. This would mean the creation of a new Ruhr district in the Brunswick countryside between Goslar and Wolfenbüttel. However, such a development would scarcely improve Salzgitter's chances of finding an individual identity. Of all the German cities, those in the Ruhr district have the biggest problems in respect of self-identification. Identifying them from outside is even harder: no German, let alone an Englishman, a Frenchman or an American, is capable of distinguishing between Bottrop and Oberhausen or Herne and Wanne-Eickel, unless he happens to have a close personal knowledge of the area. One in six major German cities is located in the Ruhr, where small towns such as Mülheim grew big, and cities such as Oberhausen emerged out of nowhere, just as Salzgitter was supposed to become a major city. The Ruhr district had coal, and next to iron ore, coal was the most important raw material for the age of industry which dawned in the nineteenth century.

The entire Ruhr district is really a single vast city, a monster industrial metropolis, 100 kilometres long and 30 kilometres wide, on which 2,000,000 tons of dust fall every year and where the sun consequently shines for a month less than the average in the rest of West Germany. But it is here that more than half the coal is mined for the countries of the European Steel and Coal Union and more than a third of Europe's steel is made, using iron ore from Lorraine and Sweden.

If Dortmund were not at the edge of the Ruhr, it would have no difficulty in maintaining its identity: 600 years ago, it was already a prosperous commercial town. But as things stand, Dortmund owes a considerable debt of gratitude to Wilhelm Overbeck, who copied the art of brewing beer from the brewers of Munich. Beer and Borussia and the vast Westfalenhalle stadium prop up the city's identity and self-esteem. For those who are ignorant of such things, I should explain that Borussia Dortmund is a football club. The quality of football in the Ruhr district is alleged to be particularly high, and one of the probable reasons for this is that each of the clubs in the area strives with missionary zeal to alert people to the identity of one of the all too many cities which are crammed together, scarcely distinguishable from one another, in this industrial region.

Compared with the Ruhr, the identity of Bonn appears relatively secure. Bonn is a small, friendly town on the Rhine which was granted a university by the Prussian king Friedrich Wilhelm III. The purpose of this was to win the sympathy of the recalcitrant Catholic Rhinelanders and make them more amenable to their new Protestant masters. The university took on a greater significance than anyone originally anticipated. It became a centre of excellence for classical and Romance philology, and it also established the first major chemical research institute, where Friedrich August Kekulé discovered the ring structure of hydrocarbon molecules. Among the noted professors who taught at Bonn were Ernst Moritz Arndt, August Wilhelm Schlegel, Karl Simrock and Ernst Robert Curtius. The university's prominent students included Heinrich Heine, Friedrich Nietzsche and Karl Marx. Nevertheless, the university, which combined Prussian Protestantism with the liberal spirit of France, remained something of an alien element in the old town, the former seat of the Archbishops of Cologne. Bonn never fully identified with its university in the manner of Tübingen, Marburg or Jena. But this was a minor problem when there were only a thousand students and a hundred professors. Even if they were not fully integrated, nobody was really bothered by their presence.

In 1944 the centre of the town was completely destroyed by Allied bombing raids. Bonn had already been devastated once before, in 1689, during the War of the Palatinate Succession. The image of the peaceful, somewhat soporific idyll which attaches to Bonn and so many other small German towns is inaccurate: Bonn's rare moments of peace never lasted very long.

After the war everything was rebuilt and became bigger, if not more beautiful, than before: the town, the university and, following Konrad Adenauer's unfathomable decision in 1949, the seat of the Federal goverment. But the whole thing never really jelled. In a limited, cramped space, three separate towns emerged: a stagnating medium-sized Rhineland town, a university town whose population is continually growing, and a government city which is bursting at the seams. All three towns sought to invade the fashionable residential areas, the Venusberg and the bank of the Rhine, but otherwise they remained more or less separate. In the north there are the villas of the prosperous townspeople, set at a distance from the residential ghetto for civil servants; in the centre there is the university; and in the south one finds the government buildings, the Federal parliament, the ministries, the embassies and consulates, and the luxury hotels for distinguished guests. What are we to do with all this if Berlin is reinstated as the capital of Germany? Do we tear it all down? If the capital moves to Berlin, it will become apparent that Bonn has grown too quickly, that its three separate parts have never fused into a single entity. Bonn will look the way it always does in the holiday periods when the students and professors, the members of parliament and the government employees have departed. As the visitor immediately realizes on arriving at what must be the world's most provincial big-city railway station, Bonn is really a quiet small town, with a vast and largely redundant appendage extending southwards from the Koblenzer Tor. What would Konrad Adenauer make of all this if he were alive today?

The antithesis of Bonn, with its three towns which refused to merge, is Berlin, which refused to be divided into two cities. From 1949 onwards, and especially after 1961, there was a continuing attempt to separate the traditional heart of the city, in the east, from the remainder in the west. The strength of the sense of collective individuality which characterizes many German cities is indicated by the fact that, despite the wall which stood for 28 years, it still remained possible to see Berlin as a single city: nobody in either the east or the west ever thought, for example, of giving a new name to the part of Berlin which they claimed as their own.

As history has shown, Germany is almost infinitely divisible. The ever-recurring division between north and south took place virtually automatically, and we have seen that it is also possible to establish an effective dividing line between east and west. Within a mere 40 years, the (Upper) Saxons became largely estranged from the Lower Saxons, and vice versa. Yet Berlin proved far more resistant, not because it was the former capital of the Reich, or because the Berliners are a particularly heroic people, but because German cities – unlike most cities in America or Asia – are highly organized, even organic, entities. They are given life by centres of energy whose functions are comparable to those of biological organs, and they require traffic "arteries", a term which in this context is more than just a metaphor.

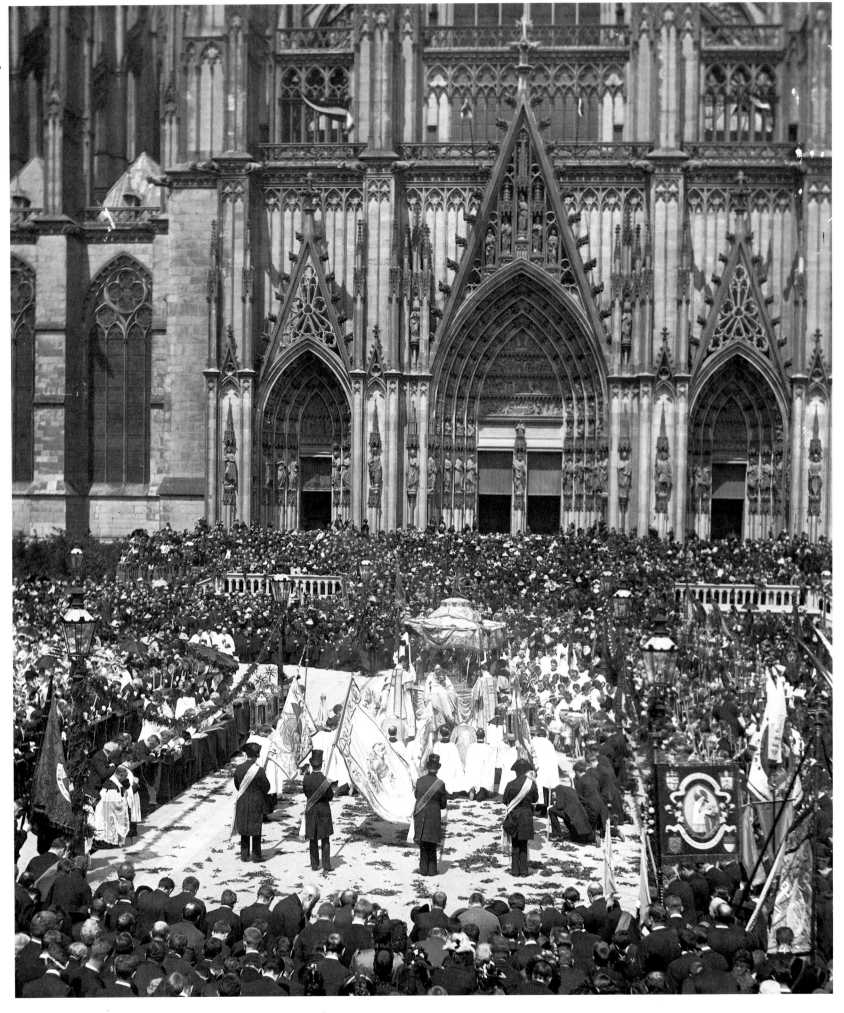

An open-air ceremony in the square at the south side of Cologne Cathedral (1891). In the nineteenth century, the Cathedral became a national monument, a symbol of the German striving for unity. A grand festival was held to mark the completion of the building in 1880.

**On the Moselle
and Main**

Exhibition centre, Frankfurt am Main
The opening of the "Galleria" caused quite a stir; the current attraction of Frankfurt's old-established exhibition centre, it is an airy glass construction linking the individual sections of the centre.

Frankfurt am Main
City of bankers and nightmare metropolis for some, for others it is the symbol of modern architecture and of where the future lies. Glittering towers of glass, steel and concrete are to be found side by side with tree-lined streets from the turn of the century.

Zell an der Mosel
The famous wine-growing village of Zell is located in a picturesque loop of the river.

Cochem an der Mosel
Lovingly restored half-timbered houses line the market-place of Cochem an der Mosel.

Trier
The bustling Moselle town of Trier can look back on more than two thousand years of history as a residence of Roman emperors and a seat of kings and bishops.

Bernkastel-Kues an der Mosel
Romantic half-timbered houses in Bernkastel-Kues, the birthplace of the Renaissance philosopher Nikolaus Cusanus, whose work is a synthesis of Scholasticism, Neo-Platonism and Humanism.

Cochem an der Mosel
Next to "Father Rhine", the Moselle is perhaps the most "German" river: View of the Moselle from the castle in Cochem, one of the region's most famous wine-growing towns.

By the Moselle
Still life with vineleaves.

Hence although Germany was partitioned in 1949, it took another twelve years to divide Berlin, and even then, the division was only possible by agreeing to leave the major arteries intact. For example, the West Berlin U-Bahn ran under East Berlin, and the S-Bahn, belonging to the East, ran through the West. However you slice up an organism, lengthways or widthways, the result is the same: if cities really were living organisms, division would kill them. Had a historian been on hand, it might at least have been possible to persuade the occupying powers to divide Berlin along the traditional boundary, instead of according to the points of the compass from which the Allied armies had marched into the city. If this had been done, Tempelhof would have been in the eastern sector, and Pankow in the west.

The city has its origins in two fishing villages, called Berlin and Köln, on the River Spree. They were amalgamated by Friedrich I in 1709, by which time they had grown into what, by the standards of the day, were substantially-sized towns. After 1871, when Berlin became Germany's first city with a population of over 1,000,000, it became impossible to see the joint between the two halves. Bismarck made Berlin the imperial capital. In the west and especially in the south of Germany, the city was less than popular; the people of Cologne, Hamburg and Munich were reluctant to acknowledge its existence. The expansion of Berlin was made possible by the reserves of energy in the east. Saxons who wanted to get on in the world went to Berlin, and it was said that every second Berliner was born in Breslau. An essential factor in the growth of the city was the liberal, tolerant attitude of the Prussian monarchs, who accepted all kinds of people – Silesians, Slavs, Saxons, Huguenots from France, and Jews – as citizens of Berlin, on the sole proviso that the immigrants were prepared to abide by the laws of the land.

Berlin has proved, if proof was ever necessary, that cities are indivisible. East Berlin is still different from West Berlin. But if one digs a short way below the surface of East Berlin, with its monumental architecture and rows of prefabricated high-rise apartments, or if one scrapes away a little of the American varnish covering the West, it immediately becomes apparent that Alexanderplatz and Kurfürstendamm still remain parts of the same city, organs belonging to the same organism.

The Cultural Life of Germany

From 1871 until 1945, Berlin had been both the political and the cultural capital of Germany. Thus when the city was divided, between 1945 and 1989, it was often said that the intellectual and artistic life of Germany had come to a standstill. I disagree with this view. On the contrary: the cultural vitality of Germany in past centuries can be seen as stemming precisely from the fact that the country lacked a metropolis, unlike Britain or France, where artists, writers and musicians flocked to London and Paris, and provincial cities such as Birmingham or Marseilles became cultural wastelands. One could also argue that during its happily brief period of prominence as the capital of Germany, Berlin never acquired the same kind of status as London or Paris, and hence that the decline of German cultural life – if it has indeed declined – has nothing to do with the partition of the former capital.

The conflict of opinions between the cultural federalists and the centralists is impossible to resolve, since "culture" in the modern sense is no longer a unified concept: it has a variety of different meanings, depending on whether we are talking about art or science, film or literature, classical philology or nuclear physics. In some cases, the concentration of resources in one place has a productive effect, in others, it inhibits cultural development. The withering of culture in the provinces would be too high a price to pay for having a thriving intellectual and artistic scene in the metropolis. On the other hand,

Less than 100 years ago, the post in parts of Germany was still delivered on horseback: the photograph shows a Bavarian postman with his horse in about 1895, fifteen years after the opening of Germany's first telephone exchange in Berlin.

the excessive fragmentation of cultural production often leads to parochialism.

Having said this, it must be admitted that a considerable shift of perspective has taken place. It would have taken Goethe between ten and twelve hours to travel by stage-coach from Weimar to Berlin, which would have meant crossing up to four borders, depending on the route: today, the journey can be done by aeroplane in half an hour. If a citizen of Berlin wanted to see the latest play at the court theatre in Weimar, he had to make the same arduous pilgrimage: nowadays, thanks to television, he can see the performance live in his own home. But do such changes constitute an argument in favour of or against cultural centralism?

Goethe's scribe and companion Eckermann records the following statement by his eminent friend:

"What else makes Germany great but the admirable popular culture which has pervaded every part of the Empire? But surely it is from the individual courts that this culture emanates; it is they who uphold and nurture it...Think of towns such as Dresden, Munich, Stuttgart, Kassel, Brunswick and Hannover...think of their influence on the neighbouring provinces and ask yourself whether all this would have happened if these towns had not been the seats of princes?" Goethe does not actually mention Weimar here, but it would of course have been well towards the top of his list of major cultural centres. It would be difficult to imagine Goethe and Schiller, Haydn and Beethoven, or Dürer and Riemenschneider, in Berlin. A homogenous region with a healthy economy probably offers the most favourable conditions for the growth of culture. A further, highly significant factor in

Road workers near Cologne (ca 1910). With the advent of the car, the construction of an efficient road system became essential.

German cultural history was the ever-available opportunity for artists to escape from political oppression or personal difficulties by simply crossing the border into the next principality, where people still spoke the same language.

For centuries, German culture flourished precisely because Germany did not exist as a political entity and had no capital city. It developed a kind of identity, but one which is less tangible and readily recognizable than that of a political unit. Yet people talk of "German" music as a distinct, coherent tradition, extending from Bach and Handel at least to Mozart and Beethoven, and possibly to Weber, Wagner and Anton von Webern. Referring to this tradition, Friedrich Nietzsche commented on what he saw as the dangers facing the Germans "from everything which stultifies the intellectual faculties and unleashes the emotions (for example the excessive use of music and strong drink)", while Thomas Mann characterized the relationship of the Germans to the world as "abstract and mystical, which is to say musical".

Reading these words today, with the mainly Anglo-American rock and pop music favoured by my children blaring away in the background, I find myself growing sceptical about even this seemingly central feature of the German character. I begin to wonder to what extent I and my countrymen can still claim any real share in the heritage of these composers: the cantor of St. Thomas's Church in Leipzig, who was born in Eisenach; the violinist from Halle who made his name as a court composer in London; the two Austrians, one of whom was only really discovered in London, and the other in Prague; the Dutchman who happened to be born in Bonn and

Franconia

Old Town Hall, Bamberg
The Old Town Hall, originally Gothic and later rebuilt in the Baroque style, stands on an island in the river Pegnitz and has survived the centuries unscathed.

The Residenz, Würzburg
Completed in about 1750 under Bishop Arnold von Schönburg, the Residenz in Würzburg is the supreme masterpiece of German Baroque architecture, unrivalled in its glorification of the system of absolute rule.

Nuremberg
The Heilig-Geist-Spital in Nuremberg was built in 1339 over a branch of the river Pegnitz; later in the 14th century, further hospitals were founded in this, the wealthiest mercantile town of the Middle Ages.

Bamberg Cathedral
The Cathedral in Bamberg is intimately connected with the Hohenstaufen emperors. Its Romanesque outline quickly came under the influence of French Gothic.

Würzburg
View of the Fortress of Marienberg above the university and cathedral town of Würzburg.

Marienberg Fortress, Würzburg
In a commanding position above the town stands the Marienberg Fortress, which was extended in the 16th and 17th centuries in connection with the Counter-Reformation.

Rothenburg ob der Tauber
This medieval town where time has stood still is nothing less than an open-air museum. Over half a million tourists come here every year from all over the world to experience German history for themselves.

Rothenburg ob der Tauber
Rothenburg's completely preserved ramparts are a powerful symbol of the medieval town as guardian of its inhabitants, personal safety and judicial rights.

then moved to Vienna; the young man from Eutin who went first to Salzburg, then to Vienna and Prague, and finally found acclaim in Dresden; the Saxon who made his fortune in Bavaria; and the founder of the Viennese School, which was essentially Austrian rather than German. It would seem that any attempt to bolster the Germans' sense of identity by reference to music is bound to run up against considerable problems.

But is there any point in testing the abstract notion of "German music" by looking at its factual basis, asking where composers were born and where they made their careers? Are such details really pertinent? I think the answer is "yes", provided that one does not attach too much argumentative weight to them. The point is not to deny that the Germans have a particular relationship to music, but merely to show that on closer examination, this *idée reçue* raises a number of questions. Perhaps, however, one should take orchestras rather than composers as one's point of reference. In the German *Länder* there are not only more theatres and opera-houses, but also – for the time being, at least – more symphony orchestras than anywhere else in the world.

Does this stem from the particular German love of music or is it merely a consequence of the time when the country was fragmented into a multitude of small states, with every prince and every archbishop wanting his own private orchestra? Many theatres and orchestras have already folded, and the wave of closures will continue. Of the world's top five orchestras, only one is German: the Berlin Philharmonic. Among the five top conductors are an Austrian, a Frenchman, an American, possibly an Englishman and possibly a Hungarian, but not a single German. The leading singers at German opera-houses come, in the first instance, from America and England, but also from Scandinavia, Spain, Hungary and the Soviet Union: there are few really top-flight German soloists. Nevertheless, there probably is something in the notion that Germany is a particularly musical country, although it is difficult to grasp and can only be understood if one expands the concept of "Germany" to include Mozart's Austria.

After so much questioning and probing, it is something of a relief to turn to the oration of the dramatist Franz Grillparzer at the funeral of Beethoven: "We who stand here by the grave of the deceased are, in a manner of speaking, the representatives of an entire nation, of the German people as a whole, mourning the death of the celebrated half of the remains of the now-vanished splendour of our native art, of the erstwhile flowering of our patriotic culture. The hero of song in the German tongue (i.e. Franz Schubert, who died the following year) is still with us: long may he live! But the last great master of composition, the heir to the immortal fame of Händel, Bach, Haydn and Mozart, has breathed his last, and we stand weeping at the broken strings, as the melody fades away."

Combining melancholy with optimism and echoing the tone of Weimar classicism, this panegyric sounds strangely antiquated, with an underlying hint of insincerity: after all, the culture of Weimar had little sympathy for Mozart. However, Goethe had been an admirer of Beethoven, who had set Schiller's "Ode to Joy" to music. In the eighteenth and especially in the nineteenth century, there was undoubtedly a closely-meshed network of relationships between the leading minds of the period. But does this constitute something to which one can apply the general label "German culture"? And what does it mean to us today?

Try as I might, I am unable to find anything specifically "German" in the painting and sculpture of Germany. However, many astute critics have discovered such a quality in the work of Albrecht Dürer, Matthias Grünewald and Tilman Riemenschneider. This argument is convincing to the extent that there is an obvious connection between the work of these three artists and a particular urban culture unique to Germany. Theirs is an art involving the conscientious,

The modern age arrives at the Hofbräuhaus in Munich. The photograph shows a group of regulars on the final evening before the well-known beer hall closed for renovation in 1896.

painstaking application of technical skill, an art which would be unthinkable without the moral and economic support of a stable community, without a firmly established circle of assistants and admiring patrons. In addition, it is based on a slight but perceptible shift in the terms of the relationship between the artist and religion, making it possible to smuggle private concerns into treatments of religious themes: the Bürger still believes in God, but has a definite sense of worldly pride.

But after these artists, where does one look for "Germanness" in German art? One thinks of Caspar David Friedrich. Perhaps there is something especially German about his brooding landscapes, heavy with Romantic longing: his subject, after all, was the German countryside, and it is far from easy to distinguish between the motif and the spirit underlying the manner of its depiction. But Friedrich was very much an isolated figure. In the eyes of the rest of the world, German Expressionist painting, with its wild formal exaggerations` and aggressive humanist pathos, seemed more typically German than any previous school of art. But in Germany itself, Expressionism was soon condemned as "degenerate", and many pictures by its exponents were burned. The Philistines called it "un-German", a view which was embraced by many, but by no means all Germans. The Americans too call things which they dislike "un-American".

It is very difficult to identify any kind of relationship between a picture and the mentality of a nation; such connections are always tenuous and require a great deal of interpretative effort. But language, especially the language of literature, invites one to take the word "German" at face value. From the

Munich's first cement cycle-track on Schleissheimer Strasse, built in 1906. Here, Thaddäus Robl, probably the most famous cyclist of his day, won an unbroken series of victories (1906/10).

Romantic era onwards, since the time of Herder, Humboldt, the Schlegels and the Grimm brothers, one does indeed find an increasing general sense of the unity of German language and literature. The noted Romance philologist Karl Vossler wrote: "The idea of the word as the origin of all things took on a clear, literal meaning, as it became apparent that language gives the world its intellectual shape: it is only in language that reality acquires its specific complexion. With this realization it became possible to see how each people creates its own world through language." However, it remains far from clear how the peoples of Switzerland, Austria and the various Germanies contrived to create such variant worlds using the same language.

It is impossible to deny the importance of language in shaping human awareness. The insistence of some people on calling Gottfried Keller a Swiss novelist or Rainer Maria Rilke an Austrian poet still smacks of pedantry. East German writers found an interested audience in the Federal Republic, and whenever a book by a West German author was published in the East, the available copies were snapped up immediately. The activities of many Austrian and Swiss publishers would be impossible were it not for the German market. But given the much-vaunted power of language, one might ask why the Germans' sense of linguistic identity has evidently failed to link up with a social identity. The answer lies in a complex set of circumstances.

**Towns and Castles
in Baden,
Württemberg and
the Palatinate**

On the Bergstrasse
Nature in full bloom on the Bergstrasse near Heppenheim. Almond, apricot, peach and walnut trees flourish here.

Wedding party in Landau-Dammheim
Such celebrations are not yet a thing of the past. Although the number of one-person households is increasing, traditional wedding festivities are still very much alive in many localities in Germany.

Ludwigsburg Castle
Erected in 1704 to 1733 under Duke Eberhard Ludwig and largely rebuilt in the neoclassical style in about 1800, this residential palace today houses an extensive castle museum.

Solitude Castle near Stuttgart
Built in 1769 in the Rococo style, this pleasure palace was connected by a thirteen kilometre-long alley to Ludwigsburg Castle.

Karlsruhe Castle
The town's roads radiate
out from the Baroque castle.
Its extensive courtyard
is decorated with fountains.

Karlsruhe
The centre-piece of
Karlsruhe's market-place
is the fountain in memory
of Grand-Duke Ludwig.

Stuttgart
Fountains on Stuttgart's Castle Square, a peaceful pedestrian precinct in this lively city.

Tübingen
Carefully restored old houses are still the most characteristic feature of the university town of Tübingen.

Tübingen
View of Neptune's fountain in front of the Linz Dispensary in Tübingen's old town.

Heidelberg
World-famous and much-sung town on the river Neckar. Thanks to its delightful position by the Odenwald, the picturesque surroundings and the mild climate, Heidelberg is generally considered one of the most beautiful towns in Germany.

Heidelberg
The Ruprecht-Karls-Universität made this university town one of the most important centres of learning in South-West Germany.

Meersburg on Lake Constance
The Old Castle seen in the glow of the setting sun. The poet Annette von Droste-Hülshoff lived here for some years.

Mainau Island, Lake Constance
Mainau Island has a reputation as a Garden of Eden; exotic fruits ripen here, and flowers bloom in gay abundance. It was first mentioned in documents in 1241 under the name of "Maginowe".

A Peaceful Revolution

The question of Germany's identity cannot be simply answered by positing the existence of a cultural Germany with a common denominator more readily found than in geographical, sociological, economic or political spheres. Nor is the solution of the problem rendered any easier by the fact that the two parts of the divided Germany have now been given the opportunity to reunite. Many people in the West welcomed the collapse of the GDR, a highly disagreeable state which towards the end of its existence was only held together by the terror tactics of the all-powerful state security police, and which was bound to break apart at the seams when the Soviet Union gave up defending its borders. But West Germans are only gradually beginning to realize that the end of the GDR also means the end of the Federal Republic, an economically powerful but otherwise small and peaceful country which was securely integrated into western Europe.

On the whole, people in the Federal Republic were reasonably happy and contented. But life in the GDR, too, was by no means as miserable as it is often represented in retrospect. The two states existed side by side, entirely separate from one another, for forty years, longer than the Weimar Republic and Hitler's Third Reich put together. Today, a new state is once more taking shape: a state which lacks a historical model and whose traditions, insofar as it has any, are fragile and unreliable.

The Holy Roman Empire, which broke up at the end of the eighteenth century, was not a state but a variegated accumulation of kingdoms, dukedoms, archbishoprics, free Imperial cities and so forth, with the symbolic figure of the Emperor at its head. However, some of the Empire's constituent parts – Bavaria, for example, and the free Hanseatic city of Hamburg – were such powerful, self-contained units that they still survive today.

The first German state was Bismarck's Second Empire, which was created by the sword and died by the sword: it lasted a mere forty-seven years. The Weimar Republic, which was forced to relinquish Alsace-Lorraine, Poznán and West Prussia, existed for fifteen years. The Third Reich, which was supposed to last for a thousand years, survived for just twelve years, and that was twelve years too many.

For the first four years after the end of the Second World War, both East and West Germany were governed by the occupying powers. This was the last time that Germany had anything like a sense of unity, arising from the resentment of the humiliated population at the often arrogant manner in which they were treated by the victorious allies. There was a general feeling of solidarity between the *Trümmerfrauen*, the women who cleared away the rubble in the devastated cities, the prisoners of war returning from the camps, and the people who lived among the ruins, with little food and no heating; the well-fed peasants, on the other hand, were frequently seen as enemies rather than allies. In Cologne, which had been completely destroyed, a new national anthem emerged, entitled "Wir sind die Eingeborenen von Trizonesien" (We Are the People of Trizonia), which was sung with great fervour during the Carnival season and at other times as well. "Trizonia" was the forerunner of the Federal Republic, made up of the three western occupation zones, which were rapidly fusing into a single state.

At the same time the Soviet zone became the GDR. For many years, politicians and political theorists debated whether, prior to the currency reform in 1948, it might have been possible to reunite the four occupation zones to create a new state, as happened in Austria. This was opposed by Konrad Adenauer and by all four occupying powers. But if a referendum had been held, at least 90 per cent of the German people would have voted in favour of reunification.

There was no referendum in 1989/90 either. There would undoubtedly have been a majority in favour of reunification, but the result would have

The musty, academic atmosphere of these artists' studios is typical of the Munich art world at the turn of the century.
Left: August Mantlich, who drew caricatures for the humorous magazine *Fliegende Blätter*.
Right: The genre painter Therese Rikoff (ca 1900).

been less clear-cut than at the end of the 1940s. The initial enthusiasm soon died down. Once again, there is a state which can be called "Germany", but the identity of the Germans still remains confused. The sixteen German *Länder* include firmly established units such as Bavaria and Saxony, and creations such as Saxony-Anhalt and Rhineland-Palatinate which emerged more or less by chance. It is surely a good thing that these regions can now live together in peace, free of political pressures, with each individual *Land* making its own distinctive contribution to the whole. But the question remains what this "whole" is supposed to be.

In his highly perceptive book *Change and Habit*, the British cultural historian Arnold Toynbee wrote: "Of the three post-Christian ideologies, individualism, Communism and nationalism, the latter has proved the most powerful." As early as 1966, Toynbee prophetically pointed to the weakness of Communism and emphasized the continuing importance of nationalism. This is an insight which we cannot afford to ignore: every time we pick up a newspaper or look at the television, we find fresh examples which confirm Toynbee's analysis.

However, there is a problem here for the new Germany, which cannot allow itself to become nationalistic. Apart from the fact that nationalism is an inappropriate attitude for a nation so unsure of itself, German nationalism wreaked so much havoc between 1871 and 1945 that it would no longer be tolerated by the world's major powers.

The peaceful revolution which broke out in the GDR on November 9, 1989 was made possible by the Soviet Union under the leadership of Mikhail Gorba-

A radical artistic innovation: plein-air painting in the countryside around Dachau. A very junior assistant patiently stands holding the sunshade over the painter and her easel (1900/10).

chev. Before these events obliged the Germans to rethink their position, the citizens of the Federal Republic were determined to play their part in building a new Europe which would ensure the continuation of a civilization that has lasted for 2,000 years. The reunification of West and East Germany is an unforeseen obtrusion in this process: despite all avowals to the contrary, it is an obstacle to the creation of a Europe which otherwise would have had a strong western bias.

What we call "Europe" originated in Greece and Rome, in France, Britain and Spain. Parts of Germany, west of the Rhine and south of the Danube, were also involved in its creation. In the second millenium of its existence, it expanded to include the German regions east of the Rhine and north of the Danube. But in the present situation we would do well to remember that for 1,000 years, the making of Europe was a process in which many other peoples participated, albeit to varying degrees: Hungarians, Czechs, Slovaks, Serbs, Croats, Lithuanians, Latvians, Estonians, Poles, Russians, Ukrainians, Romanians and Bulgarians. To bring all these nationalities together again would be a highly worthwhile undertaking, in which the geographical position of Germany, which has so often been a curse, might, for once, turn out to be a blessing.

Perhaps we do not quite understand what "Germany" really is. But in a book such as this, we can see it for ourselves: Germany is here in these photographs. Pictures often tell us more than the exercise of abstract logic. We should remember the elephant: nobody can define it, but everybody knows one when they see one.

**In Upper and
Lower Bavaria**

The Bavarian Forest near Zwiesel
This area remains relatively untouched by human hand but is attracting holiday-makers with increasing success.

Passau
The old cathedral town of Passau lies at the confluence of the rivers Danube, Ilz and Inn, and traces its history back to the celtic village "Boiodurum".

Walhalla near Donaustauf
In the commemorative temple on the wooded slopes above the Danube near Donaustauf, King Ludwig I collected busts and plaques honouring illustrious Germans.

The Water-Gap of the Danube near Weltenburg
The Abbey of the same name is a Rococo masterpiece by the Asam brothers and is situated near the spot where the Danube penetrates the southern Franconian Alps.

Liberation Monument, Kelheim
To commemorate the "Wars of Liberation", the Bavarian King Ludwig I charged the architects Klenze and Gärtner with the construction of a rotunda west of Kelheim.

Sankt Bartholomä, Königssee

Deeply recessed between the Watzmann and Hagen mountains lies the deep blue Königssee; the small pilgrimage church of St. Bartholomew was built at the end of the 17th century on the model of Salzburg Cathedral.

Karlsplatz, Munich
Affectionately known locally as "Stachus" after the owner of a former inn.

Near Garmisch-Partenkirchen
Elaborately decorated house in Upper Bavaria.

Farchant near Garmisch-Partenkirchen
The cemetery on a peaceful Sunday.

Garmisch-Partenkirchen
Situated in the valley
of the Loisach at the foot
of the Zugspitze.

Near Wildbad Kreuth
A typically Bavarian pursuit
in the summer months is
to meet in the beer garden.

Wies Church, Steingaden
A panoramic view of the famous fresco on the ceiling of the Wies Church.

Near Berchtesgaden
An idyllic scene in the Bavarian countryside with the Watzmann.

Near Ascholding
The Chapel of St. George dates from the second half of the 19th century.

Near Garmisch-Partenkirchen
Winter in Upper Bavaria with snowed-in haylofts.

Ettal Abbey near Oberammergau
This famous abbey was erected in 1330 by Ludwig the Bavarian.

Neuschwanstein Castle near Füssen
The Bavarian Ludwig II's dream of a fairy castle and also his financial ruin.

Zugspitze
The highest point in Germany: soaring to 2963 metres, the Zugspitze is able to offer year-round skiing.

Einigkeit und Recht und Freiheit
Für das deutsche Vaterland –
Danach laßt uns alle streben
Brüderlich mit Herz und Hand!
Einigkeit und Recht und Freiheit
Sind des Glückes Unterpfand.
Blüh im Glanze dieses Glückes,
Blühe deutsches Vaterland!

Hoffmann von Fallersleben 1841
The third verse of Hoffmann's song has been the German national anthem since 1952.

APPENDIX

Map
Index
List of Sources
and Illustrations

A relief map of Germany from the Alps to the North Sea and the Baltic.

Index

Numbers in italics refer to photographs.

A

Aachen 119, 129
Adenauer, Konrad 21, 105, 187, 234, 273
Adige, river 21, 22
Ahaus 109
Ahlbeck *41*
Ahrenshoop
  fishermen's cottages *45*
Allied Control Council 117
Alsace-Lorraine 105, 273
Altefähr
  Church *44*
Altenau 166
Altenburg 117
Altes Land *56,* 189
Altona 129
America 50, 62
American zone 91
Amrum, island *13, 26/27, 190/191*
Andersen, Hans Christian 202
Andreä, Johann Valentin 221, 222
Andreasberg 166
Anhalt, Principality 117
anti-Semitism 62, 63
Arndt, Ernst Moritz 187, 233
Asam brothers 279
Ascholding
  Chapel of St. George *288*
Augsburg 119, 129, *216/217*
Austria 6, 21, 22, 107, 259
Autenrieth, Johann Heinrich Ferdinand von 221
Aventinus → Turmair

B

Bach, Johann Sebastian 247, 257
"Back to Hesse" movement 105
Bad Ems *230/231*
Baden 105
Baden, Grand Duchy 22, 105
Baden-Württemberg 105
Bamberg
  Cathedral 252
  Old Town Hall 249
Bansin *41*
Barmen 129
Baur, Ferdinand Christian 221
Bavaria 73, 74, 89, 106, 223, 257, 273, 274
Bavarian Forest *277*

Bavarian Palatinate 105
Bavarian postman *246*
Becker, Hermann 187
Becker, Wilhelm 187
Becker-Modersohn, Paula 18
Beelitz *63*
Beethoven, Ludwig van 246, 257
Beilstein 51, 61, 73
  Castle 61
  Carmelite Convent 61
Belt, river 21, 22
Berchtesgaden *288*
Berlin 8, 23, 49, 107, 117, 129, 147, 234, 246
  Alexanderplatz *169,* 245
  Brandenburg Gate 8, *172/173*
  Cathedral of St. Hedwig *80/81, 84/85, 170/171*
  Charlottenburg Castle *78/79*
  "Europa Center" *77*
  Friedrichstrasse 37
  Friedrich Werder Church *80/81*
  Hitzigstrasse 147
  Kaiser-Wilhelm Memorial Church *77*
  Karl-Marx-Allee *80/81*
  Kurfürstendamm 147, 245
  Lehrter Bahnhof 37
  Lennéstrasse 147
  Nikolaiviertel *84/85*
  Pankow 245
  Palace of the Republic *80/81*
  Pankow 245
  Pariser Platz *172/173*
  Philharmonic 257
  Royal Castle *170/171*
  Schlesischer Bahnhof 37
  Spree, river *84/85*
  St. Mary's Church *170/171*
  St. Nicholas's Church *84/85*
  television tower *80/81, 84/85*
  Tempelhof 245
  Town Hall *84/85*
  Zoo station 37
Bernkastel-Kues *241*
Binz *162/163*
Bismarck, Otto von 6, 7, 21, 107, 245, 273
Bitterfeld 37, 117,
  "Bitterfeld resolutions" 37
  "Bitterfelder Weg" 37
Bloch, Ernst 222
Boisserée, Sulpiz 187, 201
Bonn 105, 187, 233, 234
  Federal Parliament 187,

234
  Koblenzer Tor 234
  market square *226/227*
  University 234
  Venusberg 234
Borchert, Wolfgang 147
Bottrop 233
Brandenburg 106
Brandenburg Gate 8
Braunshorn, Johann von 51
Bremen 73, 129, 130, *154/155*
  Roland statue *20*
Brenz, Johann 221
Breslau 245
Britain 22, 50, 275
Brodau
  river view *33*
Brunswick 22, 129, 246
  Duchy of 91
  father and daughter (1913) *91*
Burckhardt, Jakob 201
Burgsteinfurt Castle *115*
Büring, J. G. *82*

C

Camerarius, Joachim 221
Catholicism 115
Charlemagne 20
Chemnitz 117
  St. John's square *184*
  Town Hall *118*
Christian I.,
  (King of Denmark) 89
Claudel, Paul 8
Clausthal 166
Cleves 185
Coblenz 225
Cochem 61, *242/243*
collective farms 50
Cölln, August von 201
Cologne 105, 119, 129, 201, 234, 235, 245, 273, 275
  Cathedral 187, *206/207, 235*
  Church of the Assumption *206/207*
  city centre *198/199*
  Gürzenich 187
  Haymarket *205*
  Kaiserstrasse 201
  road workers *247*
  St. Martin's Church *205*
colonialism 7
communists 39, 89
Cotta, Johann Friedrich von 221

Counter-Reformation 89, 253
currency reform 273
Curtius, Ernst Robert 233

D

Dachau
  countryside *275*
Danube, river 223, 275, 279
Dauthe, J. F. C. 125
Delitzsch 37
Dessau
  Bauhaus *124*
Deutscher Bund → German League
Deutsche Reichsbahn 37
Doberan 145, 146
  Kurhaus 146
Doeberl, Michael 224
Doerbeck, B. 165
Donatello 223
Dortmund 186, 187, 233
  Alter Markt 107
  Borsigplatz 186
  Burgtor 106
  Dreikönigskirche 203
  Eving 186
  Hoesch steelworks 186
  Hohensysburg 186
  Opera *112*
  University 186
  Westfalenhalle 186, 233
Dortmund-Ems-Kanal *110*
Dresden 107, 117, 129, 202, 246, 257
  Augustus Bridge 202
  Castle Albrechtsberg *138/139*
  Castle Eckberg *138/139*
  Castle Lingner *138/139*
  Castle Moritzburg *133*
  Cavalier's House 203
  Court Church *142/143*
  Europäischer Hof 203
  Frauenkirche 203
  Grosser Garten 203
  Hofkirche 203
  Japanese Palace 203
  Kreuzkirche 203
  Museum of local history 203
  Opera 203
  Palace 203
  Semper Opera House *142/143*
  Statue of Hercules 203
  The Royal Procession *140*
  Town Hall 203
  Zwinger *141, 144,* 203

Droste-Hülshoff, Annette von 185
Duisburg
  young woman (1910) *74*
Dürer, Albrecht 246, 257
Düsseldorf 129, *228*
  Stadtgraben *208/209*

E

East Friesia 90
East Prussia 22
east-west European axis 49, 50
Eberhard Ludwig, Duke of Württemberg 264
Ebert, Friedrich 21
Eifel 61
Eisenach 247
  Wartburg Fortress *137,* 167
  Wartburg, Ceremonial Hall *137*
  Wartburg, Luther House 167
Elbe, river 37, *56,* 146, 202
Elberfeld 129
Eldena Abbey *44*
Emsland 75, 90
  Clemenswerth Hunting Lodge *146*
Ende, Edgar 18
England 50, 89
Erfurt 117, 129
  Cathedral *180*
  Petersberg *180*
  St. Severin's Church *180*
Espenhain 37, *138/139*
Ettal Abbey *289*
"Europe" 275
Eutin 257

F

Farchant
  cemetery *284*
Federal Republic of Germany (FRG) 21, 23, 37, 49, 50, 51, 73, 106, 273, 275
Feuchtwanger, Lion 165, 224
Fiesole, Mino da 223
First World War 7, 21
Flensburg
  harbour *30/31*
Fontane, Theodor 146
France 6, 7, 10, 22, 49, 50, 89, 105, 107, 275
Franconian Alps 279
Franco-Prussian War 201

Frankenhausen *126/127*
Frankfurt/Main 129, 130, 203, *238/239*
  Cathedral 203
  Eschenheim Tower 203
  Exhibition centre *237*
  Goethe's house 203
  Römerberg 203
  Zeil 203
Frankfurt/Oder 89
  Town Hall *174/175*
French-occupied zone 91
Frederick the Great 62, 83
Freiburg 105
Friedrich I. (King of Prussia) 245
Friedrich August III. (King of Saxony) 38, 107
Friedrich, Caspar David 44, 46, 257
Friedrich Franz, Grand Duke 145, 146
Friedrich Wilhelm III. (King of Prussia) 233
Friedrich Wilhelm IV. (King of Prussia) 187
Fuchs, Leonhart 221
Fuchs, Peter 201
Fugger family 216
Fulda
  St. Michael's Chapel *102/103*
furor teutonicus 63
Füssen
  Neuschwanstein Castle *290/291*

G

Garmisch-Partenkirchen *285*
  decorated house *284*
  winter scenery *289*
Gärtner, Friedrich Ritter von 279
"Geest" 28
Gelsenkirchen *110*
German Democratic Republic (GDR) 8, 21, 23, 37, 49, 50, 51, 106, 107, 273, 274
German League 6, 22
Gladbeck *111*
Glücksburg
  Castle *29*
Goethe, Johann Wolfgang von 6, 167, 187, 246, 257
Gorbatchow, Mikhail 275
Görres, Johann Joseph von 187
Goslar 166, 233
  Imperial Palace *96*

296

Gotha
  Schlossberg *182/183*
Göttingen 166
  Gänseliesel fountain *94/95*
  St. John's Church *94/95*
  Town Hall *94/95*
  University 166
Great Britain 10
Greece 275
Greetsiel *16/17*
Greifswald 107, 234
  Town Hall *38*
  University 107
Grillparzer, Franz 257
Grimm, Jakob Ludwig Karl 259
Grimm, Wilhelm Karl 259
Groitzsch 37
Gropius, Walter 124
Grün, Max von der 187
Gründerzeit 129
Grünewald, Matthias 257
Guelphs, the (dynasty) 91, 97
Güstrow 66
  Borwin Fountain *160*
  Castle *71*
  Ernst Barlach Memorial *72*
  Horse Market *160*
  St. Mary *160*

H

Halberstadt
  Cathedral *181*
  Fish Market *181*
  St. Martin's Church *181*
Halle 117, *119*, 129, 247
Halligen *29*
Hamburg 37, 73, 89, 129, 130, 146, 147, 245,
  Alster 146
  Binnenalster *54/55*
  harbour *23, 53, 152/153*
  Jungfernstieg *150/151*
  Mönckebergstrasse 73
Hamme, river 147
Händel, Georg Friedrich 119, 247, 257
Hanover 129, 246
  Herrenhausen Castle *156/157*
  Hohes Ufer *158/159*
Hanover, Kingdom of 22, 91
Hanseatic cities 51, 130, 273
Hanseatic League 42, 73
Harzburg 166
Harz Mountains 96, 97, 117, 166

Bode Valley *96*
  Herzberg Castle *97*
Hauff, Wilhelm 221
Hausenstein, Wilhelm 221
Haydn, Joseph 21, 246, 257
Hegel, Georg Friedrich Wilhelm 221, 222
Heidelberg 222, *269*
  Castle *222*
  University *269*
Heiliger Damm 146
Heine, Heinrich 166, 187, 234
Heinrich VII., Emperor 51, 61
Helgoland *14/15,* 145
Hell, river 167
Heppenheim, Bergstrasse *261*
Hercynian Mountains 92
Kelheim
  Liberation Monument 279
Herder, Johann Gottfried 6, 259
Heringsdorf *41*
Hesse 91, 106
Hesse-Darmstadt 105
Hesse-Nassau 105
Heuss, Theodor 21
Hitler, Adolf 7
Hoffmann von Fallersleben 21, 22, 23, 145, 293
Hölderlin, Friedrich 6, 221, 222
Holl, Ludwig 50
Holland 185, 187
Holocaust 7
Holstein 106
Holsteinische Schweiz *33*
Holy Roman Empire 10, 119, 130, 273
Hörsel Mountains 167
"Horst Wessel Song" 21
Huch, Ricarda 185, 221
Humboldt, Wilhelm von 259
Hunsrück 61
Husum 28

I

idyllic scene *90*
industrialization 7
Iron Curtain 50

J

Jena 117, 234
Jens, Walter 222
Jews 7, 62
Johann the Younger, Duke 29
Jüterbog 37

K

Kant, Immanuel 6, 146
Karl VII. (King of Sweden) 146
Karl August, Duke of Saxony-Weimar 167
Karlsruhe
  market place *265*
  castle *265*
Kassel 246
  Wilhelmshöhe Castle *100/101*
Kästner, Erich 203
Kaub am Rhein
  Gutenfels Castle *228*
  Pfalz *229*
Kekulé, Friedrich August 233
Keller, Gottfried 259
Kepler, Johannes 221
Kiel
  Kiel Fjord *149*
  "Little Kiel" *149*
Kieritzsch 37
Klenze, Leo von 279
Klosterberg 61
Knobelsdorff, G. W. von 83
König, René 119
Königssee *280/281*
  St. Bartholomä *280/281*
Krefeld 129
Krolow, Karl 167

L

Lake Constance *270/271*
Landau-Dammheim
  wedding party *262/263*
Landolfshausen *93*
Langbehn, Julius 73
Langeness, island *29*
Lautenthal 166
Lehde *86*
Leine, river 166
Leipzig 37, 49, 106, 107, 117, 129
  Alte Börse *121*
  Church of St. Nicholas 125
  Statue of Goethe *121*
  St. Thomas's Church 247
Lessing, Gotthold Ephraim 6
Leuna 37
limes 73
Lippe-Detmold, Principality 105
List, Friedrich 221
Lithuania 22
London 247

Lorraine 105, 233
Lower Pomerania 107, 117
Lower Saxony 90, 91
Lübeck 129, 130
  Holstentor *34/35*
Lübbenau 87
Luckenwalde 37
Ludwig I. (King of Bavaria) 187, 279
Ludwig the Bavarian 289
Ludwigsburg Castle *264*
Lüneburg 57
Lüneburg Heath *57*
Luther, Martin 37, 122, 124

M

Maas, river 21, 22
Mackensen, Fritz 18
Madariaga, Salvador de 49
Magdeburg 117, 129
  Cathedral *118*
  Horseman *178/179*
  Old Market *178/179*
  St. John's Church *178/179*
Main, river 75
Mainau, island *272*
Mainz 119, 129, *212/213*
Mann, Thomas 6, 192, 223, 247
Mantlich, August *274*
Marburg an der Lahn *104,* 234
Mark Brandenburg 37
"Marsch" *28, 29*
Marx, Karl 39, 234
Maximilian II., Emperor 218
Mecklenburg 89, 106, 107, 117
Mecklenburg, Dukes of 68
Mecklenburg-Güstrow, Dukes of 71
Mecklenburg Lakelands *64*
Mecklenburg-Schwerin, Grand Duchy 22, 107
Mecklenburg-Strelitz 107
Meersburg *270/271*
Meissen 117, 202
  Albrecht Fortress *134/135*
  Cathedral *134/135,* 202
  market square *134/135*
Memel, river 21, 22
Merseburg 117, *128*
  Cathedral *125*
  Merseburger Zaubersprüche 125
Metternich, Klemens Wenzel, Prince of 61, 187
Modersohn, Otto 18
Mohr, Christian 201

Moller, Georg 201
Montabaur 105
Montabaur, district of 91
Moscow 48, 89
Moselle, river 61, 62, *244*
Moselle valley 61, 117
Mozart, Wolfgang Amadeus 247, 257
Mülheim 233
Munich 129, 222, 245, 246
  Cathedral *220*
  Hofbräuhaus *258*
  Karlsplatz *282/283*
  Ludwigstrasse 223
  Marienplatz *220*
  Maximilianstrasse *218/219*
  National Theatre *218/219*
  Oktoberfest beer tent *194/195*
  Residence 222
  Schleißheimer Strasse 259
  St. Peter's Church *220*
Münster 185
  Buddenturm 185
  Cathedral *116*
  Zwinger 185
Münsterland 75, 167, 186
Müritz, lake *67, 70*
  Castle Klink *65*

N

Napoleon Bonaparte 61, 105, 117, 130
Napoleonic Wars 6
national anthem 21, 293
National Socialism 7
Nazis 38, 39
Neckar, river 222
Neckar gorge 222
neo-classical architecture 50
Neu-Schulenburg 166
Neustadt in Holstein *28*
Nietzsche, Friedrich 6, 247
Nitzscha 37
Nordkirchen Castle *114*
North Friesland *28, 29*
North German League 145
North Rhine-Westphalia 49, 105, 117
North Sea
  wicker beach chairs *11*
Nuremberg 119, 129, 130, 221
  Castle Tower 221
  Christmas Market *196/197*
  Executioner's Bridge 221
  fleamarket 221
  Fleischbrücke 221
  Heilig-Geist-Spital *252*

St.-Ägidius-Kirche 221

O

Oberhausen 233
Oberwesterwald 105
Oder, river 107
Oeser, A. F. 125
Oker-Reservoir 166
Oldenburg 185
Oldenburg, Duchy of 91
Overbeck, Wilhelm 18, 233

P

Paris 49
Parliament at the Paulskirche 6
Passau
  Donaustauf *278*
  Walhalla *278*
Pegnitz, river 221
Permoser, Balthasar *144*
Philip the Generous, Duke 91
Pictorius, Gottfried Laurenz 114
Poland 22, 107
Pomerania 146
"Portrait of Europe" 49
Potsdam 117, 165
  Bassinplatz 165
  Berlin Gate 165
  Charlottenstrasse 165
  Chinese Tea-House *82*
  Glienicke Bridge 165
  Sanssouci Palace *82, 83,* 221
  Wilhelmplatz 165
Poznán 273
Prague 247
Preller the Younger, Friedrich 167
Protestantism 74, 75, 105, 131, 221
Prussia 22, 62, 89, 91, 107, 117, 170

R

Ramboux, Johann J. 187, 201
"Realpolitik" 10
Reformation 89, 107
Regensburg 119, 129
regional costumes (1911) *51*
Revolution (1918) 89
Reuss, house of 117
Rhine, river 145, 187, 224, *225, 232,* 275

Rhine valley 222
Rhineland 75, 105
Rhineland-Palatinate 105, 106, 117, 274
Riemenschneider, Tilman 246, 257
Rikoff, Therese *274*
Rilke, Rainer Maria 147, 259
Roggow *66*
Roman civilization 10
Rome 275
Romkerhalle waterfall 166
Rostock 107, 129, 145
  Marienkirche *39*
  New Market *161*
  St. Nicholas *42/43*
  St. Peter *42/43*
  Town Hall *161*
  University 107
  Warnow, river *42/43*
Rothenburg ob der Tauber 51, *254/255, 256*
Rügen, island 146
  chalk cliffs *46/47*, 146
  Stubbenkammer *46/47*
Ruhr 105, 117, 118, 233
  district 233
Russia 49, 89

S

Saale, river 128
Saale valley 117
Saar, Saarland 105, 106, 118
Sächsische Schweiz (Saxon Alps)
  Bastei *140, 141*
Salzburg 221, 257
Salzgitter 130, 233
  Bad Salzgitter 130
Sauerland 186
Saxony 37, 49, 50, 51, 106, 107, 117, 274
  Saxony-Altenburg 117
  Saxony-Anhalt 89, 106, 117, 274
  Saxony-Coburg 117
  Saxony-Meiningen 117
  Saxony-Weimar-Eisenach 117
Schaumburg-Lippe, Principality 91
Schelling, Friedrich Wilhelm Joseph von 221
Schiller, Friedrich von 6, 167, 257
Schlegel, August Wilhelm 233, 259
Schlegel, Friedrich von 259

Schleswig *32*
  Gottorf Castle *32*
Schleswig-Holstein 21, 74, 89, 91, 106
  Duchy of 22
  Dukes of 32
Schneider-Clauss, Wilhelm 201
school classroom (1911) 75
Schubert, Franz 257
Schulenberg 166
Schumacher, Fritz 150
Schwarzburg-Rudolstadt 117
Schwarzburg-Sondershausen, Principality 22, 117
Schwerin
  Castle *68/69*
  Cathedral *160*
  State Theatre *160*
Schwering, Max Leo 201
Second Empire 6, 107, 201, 273
Second World War 8, 37, 50, 91, 169, 273
Senheim 61
Sichard, Johann 221
Silesia 187
Simrock, Karl 201, 233
Soest 129
"Song of the Germans" 21, 23
Sorbs (slavic population) 86
South Tyrol 21, 22
Soviet Union 37, 275
Spain 275
Spengler, Oswald 63
Spree Forest *86, 87, 176*
Spree, river 245
Stade on the Schwinge
  town houses *56*
Staël, Germaine de 167
Stalin, Josef 39
steel combines 50
Steingaden
  Wies Church *286/287*
St. Goarshausen 91
  Loreley *229*
Storm, Theodor 2
Stralsund 146
  Kütertor *39*
  Town Hall *164*
Straubing
  student (1890) *74*
Stuttgart 105, 129, 130
  Castle Square *266/267*
  Market Square *214/215*
  Solitude Castle *264*
Sweden 145
Sylt, island 22

T

Teutoburg Forest, battle of 73
Third Reich 21, 233, 273
Thirty Years War 71, 74, 89
Thuringia 117
Thuringian Forest 117, 167, 200
Tollensesee *58/59*
Toynbee, Arnold 274
Travemünde
  beach *25*
  harbour *36*
Treaty of Versailles 7
Trier 21, 119, 129, *241*
Tübingen 221, 234, *268*
  Neptune's fountain *268*
Turmair, Johann 223
Twain, Mark 222
Tyrol 21

U

Ulbricht, Walter 107
Ulm 129
Unger, Georg Christian 165
Unstrut, river 117
Unterlahn 91
Unterwesterwald 91
Usedom, island *41*

V

Verdun 21
Vienna 257
Vischer, Friedrich Theodor 221
Vischering Castle *115*
Vogeler, Heinrich 18
Voigtel, Richard 201
Vossler, Karl 253

W

Wagner, Richard 247
Wahmbeck *98/99*
Wallenstein, Albrecht Eusebius Wenzel 39, 71
Wallraf, Max 187
Walter von der Vogelweide 22
Wanne-Eickel 233
War of the Palatinate Succession 234
Waren
  Church of St. Mary *70*
  "Löwenapotheke" *70*
  New Market Square *70*
Warnemünde 145

Warnow, river 145
Warsaw 89
Wasungen
  carnival *200*
Weber, Karl Julius 146
Weber, Karl Maria von 247
Webern, Anton von 247
Weerth, Georg 202
Weimar 117, 167, 221, 246, 257
  Central Library of German Classic Literature *136*
  Court Theatre 246
  Goethe's garden house *136*
  Green Castle *136*
Weimar Republic 21, 273
Weisenborn, Günter 187
Welchert, Hans-Heinrich 145
Weltenburg *279*
Wendland, Free Republic of 90
Wernigerode *97*
  Castle *97*
Weser, river *98/99*, 147, *154/155*
  valley 147
Weserbergland *93, 98/99*
Westphalia 105, 167, 185
West Prussia 273
Wiederizsch 37
Wieland, Christoph Martin 167
Wiesbaden *210/211*
Wildbad Kreuth
  beer garden *258*
Wilhelmine Empire 129
Wismar
  actors in period dress *192/193*
  "Alter Schwede" *48*
  Market Square *48, 71*
  St. George's Church *45*
  "Wasserkunst" *48*
Wittenberg 37
  Boy's Choir *131*
  Castle Church *122/123, 124*
  market square *122/123*
  Town Hall *122/123*
Woldegk
  Windmill *60*
Wolfenbüttel 233
Worpswede 147
  forest house *18/19*
Wümme, river 147
Würzburg
  elderly lady (1913) *91*
  Marienberg Fortress 253
  Residence *250/251*

Württemberg-Baden 105
Württemberg-Hohenzollern 105
Württemberg, Kingdom 105

Z

Zell an der Mosel *240*
Zille, Heinrich 165
Zugspitze *292*
Zwiesel 275
Zwirner, Ernst 187, 201

List of Sources

Hans Christian Andersen
Pictures of Travel. New York: Hurd & Houghton, 1871.

Wolfgang Borchert
"Hamburg", in *Das Gesamtwerk*. © 1949 by Rowohlt Verlag GmbH, Hamburg.

Annette von Droste-Hülshoff
"Westfälische Schilderungen", in *Sämtliche Werke in zwei Bänden*, vol.1. Munich: Winkler Verlag, n.d.

Lion Feuchtwanger
"Berlin", in *Success: Three Years in the Life of a Province*. Trans. Willa and Edwin Muir, London: Martin Secker, 1930.

Lion Feuchtwanger
"Old Bavaria", ibid.

Theodor Fontane
"Briefe aus Mecklenburg", in *Sämtliche Werke*. Munich: Nymphenburger Verlagsbuchhandlung, 1972.

Max von der Grün
"Dortmund", in Bartle F. Sinnhuber, ed., *Hier lebe ich*. Rosenheim: Rosenheimer Verlagshaus, 1978.

Wilhelm Hausenstein
"Nürnberg", in *Besinnliche Wanderfahrten*. Munich: Verlag Schnell & Steiner, 1955. © by Margot and R.M. Parry Hausenstein.

Heinrich Heine
"The Harz", in *Heine's Pictures of Travel*. Trans. Charles Godfrey Ireland, 5th rev. ed., New York: Leypoldt & Holdt, 1866.

Georg Hermann
Spaziergang in Potsdam. Berlin: Kupfergraben Verlagsgesellschaft, 1986.

Ricarda Huch
"Frankfurt", in *Im alten Reich*. Bremen: Carl Schünemann Verlag, 1968.

Ricarda Huch
"Münster", in ibid.

Walter Jens
Die kleine grosse Stadt: Tübingen. Stuttgart: Konrad Theiss Verlag, 1981.

Erich Kästner
Gesammelte Schriften, vol.5. Zurich: Atrium Verlag, 1959.

Karl Krolow
"Bilder aus vergangenen Tagen", in *Merian-Heft* 11/XXVI. Hamburg: Hoffmann und Campe Verlag, 1973.

Thomas Mann
"Gladius Dei", in *Little Herr Friedemann and Other Stories*. Harmondsworth: Penguin, 1972. © Martin Secker & Warburg Ltd., 1961.

Mark Twain
A Tramp Abroad, vol. 1. New York: Harper & Brothers n.d.

Friedrich Preller the Younger
Eine Künstlerjugend. Weimar 1930.

Rainer Maria Rilke
"Introduction to Worpswede", in *Selected Works*, vol.1. Trans. G. Craig Houston, introd. J.B. Leishman, London: The Hogarth Press, 1954.

Max Leo Schwering
Köln 1850-1920. Lucerne, Frankfurt am Main: Verlag C.J. Bucher, 1980.

Anne Louise Germaine de Staël
Zehn Jahre meiner Verbannung. Leipzig 1822.

Carl Julius Weber
Deutschland oder Briefe eines in Deutschland reisenden Deutschen. 3rd. ed., Stuttgart: Hallberg'sche Verlagsbuchhandlung, 1855.

Georg Weerth
"Kölner Karnival", in *Sämtliche Werke,* vol. V. Berlin, Weimar: Aufbau Verlag, 1957.

Günther Weisenborn
"Bonn", in *Auf Sand gebaut*. Munich, Vienna, Basle: Verlag Kurt Desch, 1956.

Hans-Heinrich Welchert
"Roter Fels im Meer", in *Wanderungen zu den Schlössern und Domen Schleswig-Holsteins*. Frankfurt am Main: Societäts Verlag, 1978.

We are grateful to the publishers and copyright-holders for permission to reprint extracts from the above works. Despite strenuous efforts, it has not been possible in all cases to trace the copyright-holders. We would ask anyone who feels that their copyright has been infringed to contact us.

List of Illustrations

Archiv für Kunst und Geschichte, Berlin
p. 39 right, 118, 131, 177, 178/179.

Berlinische Galerie/Photographische Sammlung, Berlin
p. 169, 172/173.

Bildarchiv Bucher, Munich
p. 22, 106, 107.

Bildarchiv Foto Marburg, Marburg
p. 154/155, 2167217, 218/219, 246, 274.

Bildarchiv Preußischer Kulturbesitz, Berlin
p. 158/159, 164, 176 above

Käthe Hamann, Hamburg
p. 150/151.

Hessisches Landesmuseum, Wiesbaden
p. 210/211.

Historisches Museum Am Hohen Ufer, Hannover
p. 156/157.

Rheinisches Bildarchiv, Köln
p. 205, 206/207, 235, 247.

Sächsische Landesbibliothek, Dresden
p. 160 below, 161, 174/175, 180, 182/183, 184.

Axel Schenck Collection, Munich
p. 11, 23, 50, 51, 62, 63, 74, 75, 90, 91.

Erich Schenck Collection, Hildesheim
p. 170/171.

Sammlung Wehrli im Eidgenössischen Archiv für Denkmalpflege, Berne
p. 162/163.

Staatsarchiv Hamburg
p. 152/153.

Stadtarchiv Munich
p. 220, 258, 259.

Süddeutscher Verlag, Munich
p. 149, 212/213.

Ullstein Bilderdienst, Berlin
p. 38, 39 left, 119, 160 above, 176 below, 181, 208/209, 214/215, 275.

All remaining illustrations:
Josef H. Neumann
Josef H. Neumann used a Russian "Horizon" panoramic camera.

Map on p. 295:
© **Mairs Geographischer Verlag/Studio Berann-**

299